T0318961

Cambridge Elements

Elements in American Politics
edited by
Frances E. Lee
Princeton University

THE ACCEPTANCE AND EXPRESSION OF PREJUDICE DURING THE TRUMP ERA

Brian F. Schaffner
Tufts University

CAMBRIDGE
UNIVERSITY PRESS

University Printing House, Cambridge CB2 8BS, United Kingdom

One Liberty Plaza, 20th Floor, New York, NY 10006, USA

477 Williamstown Road, Port Melbourne, VIC 3207, Australia

314–321, 3rd Floor, Plot 3, Splendor Forum, Jasola District Centre,
New Delhi – 110025, India

79 Anson Road, #06–04/06, Singapore 079906

Cambridge University Press is part of the University of Cambridge.

It furthers the University's mission by disseminating knowledge in the pursuit of education, learning, and research at the highest international levels of excellence.

www.cambridge.org
Information on this title: www.cambridge.org/9781108927024
DOI: 10.1017/9781108924153

First published 2020

A catalogue record for this publication is available from the British Library.

ISBN 978-1-108-92702-4 Paperback
ISSN 2515–1606 (online)
ISSN 2515–1592 (print)

The Acceptance and Expression of Prejudice during the Trump Era

Elements in American Politics

DOI: 10.1017/9781108924153
First published online: October 2020

Brian F. Schaffner
Tufts University

Author for correspondence: Brian F. Schaffner, brian.schaffner@tufts.edu

Abstract: What are the consequences when politicians make prejudiced statements? Theories about the suppression of prejudice argue that people are likely to express more prejudice when they believe that norms are more permissive than they may have otherwise assumed. Using a series of experiments carried out during and since the 2016 campaign, I show that being exposed to Donald Trump's prejudiced rhetoric causes people to express more prejudice themselves. Notably, this is not merely a "Trump effect": people's commitment to anti-prejudice norms is undermined even when exposed to prejudiced rhetoric attributed to unnamed politicians. These findings are consequential: if politicians increasingly feel at liberty to express explicit prejudice, then the mass public is likely to take cues from such behavior, leading them to express more prejudice themselves. This may lead to increasingly heightened intergroup tensions that could pose a threat to political and social stability in the United States.

Keywords: prejudice, rhetoric, public opinion, motivated reasoning, partisanship

ISBNs: 9781108927024 (PB), 9781108924153 (OC)
ISSNs: 2515-1606 (online), 2515-1592 (print)

Contents

1 Introduction

In the musical *Avenue Q*, puppets controlled by human actors famously sing that "Everyone's a little bit racist, sometimes. Doesn't mean we go around committing hate crimes." It's true, for the most part. Social science research has taught us time and again that people hold more internal prejudice privately than they are willing to express to others. The reason for this is that we try to follow norms, the unwritten rules of society about what things are ok to say or do and what crosses the line. We do this because we care about both how others see us and also how we see ourselves. And we learn about these norms not only from our social circles but also from our political leaders. So what happens when our most prominent political leader repeatedly signals to us that the norms have changed? What happens when he says things that we used to think crossed a line?

In June 2015, Donald Trump began his presidential campaign with an offensive remark about Mexicans that many thought would immediately derail his aspirations. After all, he seemed to be violating long-held norms when he said, about Mexicans immigrating to the United States,

> They're bringing drugs. They're bringing crime. They're rapists. And some, I assume, are good people. But I speak to border guards and they tell us what we're getting. And it only makes common sense. It only makes common sense. They're sending us not the right people.[1]

Trump was widely criticized for these remarks at the time, but they did not drive him out of the race. Far from it. Instead, Trump went on to insult and belittle so many different people and groups during his campaign and into his presidency that the *New York Times* kept a running tally of who he had insulted, a list that had nearly hit 600 when it was last updated in May 2019.[2]

During the 2016 campaign, the Southern Poverty Law Center published a report titled "The Trump Effect," in which American teachers reported that they noticed increased bullying and harassment of students who were from racial or ethnic minority groups (Costello 2016). This study provides chilling but circumstantial evidence that Trump's rhetoric may have given some people license to express their prejudice in a way that they previously were not comfortable with. In other words, Trump may be single-handedly shifting our norms with potentially dangerous consequences for our politics and society. But is Trump's rhetoric really *causing* these things to happen? And, if so, how widespread is the "Trump effect"? Can anything be done to counteract it?

[1] See https://time.com/3923128/donald-trump-announcement-speech/.

[2] See the list at www.nytimes.com/interactive/2016/01/28/upshot/donald-trump-twitter-insults.html.

These are critical questions and they are part of a much broader conversation that has been taking place since Trump's successful campaign for president in 2016. Following the election, a litany of editorials and op-eds warned of the threat that Trump was posing to American democracy. These concerns were not limited to the editorial boards of the world's leading newspapers, however. Indeed, for many scholars who study democracy, Trump's election was the canary in the coal mine for worries about the possible eroding of democratic norms or even of democracy itself. One group of scholars launched Bright Line Watch, a project designed to track the health of (and public support for) American democratic institutions, noting, "At a time of potential danger to American democratic norms and institutions, it is more urgent than ever for scholars to highlight the risks to our system of government."[3] Among other metrics, the scholars behind this study find a significant drop in how a large sample of political scientists rated the quality of US democracy after Trump's election to office (Carey et al. 2019).

At the same time, the broad public concern about what Trump's election meant for democratic norms was evident from the fact that Steven Levitsky and Daniel Ziblatt's book *How Democracies Die* spent over a month on the *New York Times* bestseller list in 2018 (Levitsky & Ziblatt 2018). Levitsky and Ziblatt provide a sobering examination into the question of whether American democracy is in danger of eroding, warning, "Democracies work best – and survive longer – where constitutions are reinforced by unwritten democratic norms" (p. 8). The authors go on to note:

> America's efforts to achieve racial equality as our society grows increasingly diverse have fueled an insidious reaction and intensifying polarization. And if one thing is clear from studying breakdowns throughout history, it's that extreme polarization can kill democracies. (p. 9)

As I will discuss, one reason that increasing polarization is so dangerous is because it creates incentives for politicians and the mass public to abandon support for long-held democratic and societal norms. Indeed, the extreme polarization in America is at least partly fueled by the same identity politics that Trump used to capture the presidency.

Many norms are essential, but among them is mutual toleration and respect. Indeed, democratic society works best when citizens can participate in politics – and everyday life – free from the fear of being attacked for who they are or where they come from. This is why expressions of prejudice, particularly from politicians, can be so pernicious. Most politicians have at least paid lip service

[3] https://brightlinewatch.org/.

to anti-prejudice norms over the past few decades. Consider the 2008 campaign, when John McCain was booed at campaign rallies for shutting down prejudiced attacks on Barack Obama from his supporters. Or the 2012 contest, when Mitt Romney's most controversial statement was a confusing remark about having "binders full of women" – a clumsy attempt by the candidate to promote his attempts to hire women into leadership roles.

It is plain to see that Trump's behavior is a dramatic departure from that of his predecessors. And when Trump won the presidency based on the votes of 63 million Americans, it gave his many transgressions even greater weight. At worst, Trump's victory could easily be viewed as a full-throated endorsement of prejudice and misogyny by a large swath of Americans; at best, it showed that many were at least willing to tolerate such behavior. Either way, the fear is that it was a signal to many people that their own prejudiced views were not something to hide or be ashamed of but rather something that much of America would tolerate or even celebrate. Therefore, it would not be surprising to find that Trump's rhetoric has changed how some Americans express their own prejudice.

Relying mostly on four unique experiments carried out over three years, I am able to provide the strongest evidence to date not only that Trump's rhetoric can cause people to express more prejudice than they would otherwise but also that this effect is not limited to Trump himself. Specifically, I find that white Americans react to Trump's offensive rhetoric by saying more negative and offensive things, not only about the group targeted by Trump's remarks but often by commenting more negatively about other groups as well. I also find that people take normative cues even from generic politicians. But to understand why this happens, I first elaborate on what we know about prejudice, why it is often suppressed by individuals, and the circumstances under which that suppression gives way to expression.

1.1 Distinguishing between Prejudice and Its Expression

It has long been understood by scholars that there is an important difference between how much prejudice an individual holds internally and how much prejudice they express externally. In the social psychology literature, this is known as the "two-factor" theory of prejudice. As Crandall and Eshleman (2003) explain:

> These theories hypothesize that people are trying to simultaneously satisfy two competing motivations, based on (a) racial prejudice and (b) motivation to suppress prejudice. This conflict creates ambivalent emotions, behavioral instability, and cognitive inconsistency. (p. 415)

An individual's genuine (internal) prejudice develops over time, largely through a process of socialization. The key agents in this socialization process appear to be parents as well as social networks. Because much of our prejudices are ingrained in us at a young age, internally held prejudice is generally thought to be difficult to change, at least in the short term (Paluck & Green 2009).

While people hold some level of internal prejudice, they generally hide much of that prejudice from others. As Crandall and Eshleman (2003) note, "people suppress prejudice both to maintain a nonprejudiced appearance and to deny prejudice to themselves and maintain a nonprejudiced self-concept" (p. 420). In other words, people may suppress their prejudice to conform to norms about what kind of language is acceptable in a particular social situation (an external motivation), but they also may do so in order to adhere to their own standards, such as a commitment to egalitarianism (an internal motivation). What this means is that the prejudice that a person reveals in conversation or even in responses to survey questions is typically not reflective of the true prejudice that they actually hold (Roese & Jamieson 1993).

Importantly, because expressed prejudice is distinct from genuine prejudice, there is a great deal of potential for people to express more or less prejudice over time and in different situations. As a simple example, different approaches to measuring prejudice produce significantly different results. Social psychologists sometimes use a method called the "bogus pipeline" where subjects are connected to a machine and are told that the machine is able to determine what the subject actually thinks or feels. In pioneering this approach, Sigall and Page (1971) found that white subjects connected to the machine offered significantly more negative evaluations of African Americans compared to those who were not connected (and therefore believed that they could successfully mask their prejudice).

While the "bogus pipeline" approach is limited to lab-based settings, political scientists have successfully implemented list experiments on surveys in an attempt to more accurately measure prejudiced views. The list experiment is a different approach to getting people to admit to socially undesirable views and behaviors. Respondents are provided with a list of items and asked to indicate how many are true for them, but without having to identify which specific items they agree with. Half the sample receives a shorter list, while the other half receives a list with the additional item that the researchers are interested in. The difference in the average number of items that respondents say they agree with provides insight into how many agree with the item of interest. For example, Kuklinski, Cobb, and Gilens (1997) used a list experiment to find that 42 percent of southern whites would be angry if a black family moved in next door to them. This estimate was much higher than what one would glean from asking the same group of individuals explicitly about the situation.

The "bogus pipeline" and list experiment studies are just two examples of methods social scientists have used to demonstrate a simple point: people are generally more prejudiced than they care to admit to others and, sometimes, even to themselves.

1.2 When Will People Express Prejudice?

While prejudice itself is generally quite stable, peoples' willingness (or reluctance) to *express* prejudicial attitudes outwardly appears to be much more malleable (Blanchard et al. 1994; Blanchard, Lilly & Vaughn 1991; Crandall & Eshleman 2003; Paluck 2009; Zitek & Hebl 2007). Social conformity has long been thought to play an important role not only in the extent to which individuals hold prejudicial attitudes but also in the extent to which they express those attitudes to others (Allport 1954). For the most part, there has been a clear social norm in the United States regarding the expression of prejudice toward people of other races and ethnicities for many decades (Dovidio & Gaertner 1986; Rokeach & Ball-Rokeach 1989). This is evident from the fact that expressions of prejudice toward racial and ethnic minority groups dropped sharply since the middle of the twentieth century, even though unobtrusive measures reveal that actual prejudice has not declined nearly as much (Crosby, Bromley & Saxe 1980; Hurwitz & Peffley 1992; Kuklinski et al. 1997). Thus, it seems that at least part of the reason people express less prejudice toward minority racial groups is to conform to social norms that discourage such speech.

While some level of suppression of prejudice is a default state for most people, justifications offer a release from this suppression. As Ford, Boxer, Armstrong, and Edel (2008) put it, "Justifications allow people to express an otherwise suppressed prejudice without feeling self-directed negative affect (e.g. guilt, shame) or fearing negative social sanctions" (p. 160). For example, Blanchard et al. (1994) allowed research subjects to overhear another subject's responses to questions related to racism before they themselves answered the same questions. However, the ostensibly overheard responses were actually given by a confederate – an individual working with the researchers – whose remarks were randomly assigned. When the subject overheard remarks from the confederate condoning racism, that subject was also more likely to condone it, and when a subject overheard the confederate condemning racism, he or she was more likely to also express condemnation. This finding has been replicated by several similar studies focusing on a variety of different types of prejudice (Blanchard et al. 1991; Zitek & Hebl 2007).

Social psychologists have also studied how being exposed to prejudiced humor can lead people to express more prejudice themselves (Ford et al. 2008). For example, with regard to sexist humor, Ford, Wentzel, and Lorion (2001) explain that, "by communicating derision of women in a light-hearted or jovial manner, sexist humor expands the bounds of appropriate conduct in the immediate context" (p. 678). In other words, because prejudiced humor is seen by many as a normative gray area, exposure to such humor makes people more likely to express their own prejudices.

Of course, it is natural to assume that citizens have differing conceptions of what is or is not acceptable when it comes to expressing prejudice. It is also reasonable to imagine that some people are more confident about what these norms are compared to others. Indeed, this variance and uncertainty reflects the fact that norms are often ambiguous and vary significantly across different situations and contexts. Accordingly, as the experiments described earlier show, people rely on cues from others regarding what the norms are in any particular situation (Cialdini & Trost 1998). Cues can also come from sources beyond an individual's peer network. For example, Paluck (2009) finds that radio programs are effective in providing signals about norms related to prejudice. The study involved randomizing the types of radio programs that individuals in Rwanda were exposed to, with the aim of examining the impact of a program that focused on themes of ethnic reconciliation. Notably, being exposed to the anti-prejudice program did not affect listeners' actual beliefs about out-groups, but they did affect their perceptions of norms regarding the acceptability of openly engaging in prejudicial behavior. Furthermore, by affecting listeners' perceptions of social norms, their behavior was altered. That is, people exposed to the anti-prejudice program behaved in a less prejudiced way, even though they had not become less prejudiced.[4]

1.3 Can Political Rhetoric Lead to More Expressed Prejudice?

Overall, it is clear that people do take cues from peers or even media programs when deciding the appropriate way to behave when it comes to expressing their biases toward out-groups. Based on this literature and what we know about elite influence in general, it is reasonable to assume that political elites would also be able to send influential signals about the appropriate norms regarding expressions of prejudice. After all, the large body of scholarship on framing, priming, and agenda setting has demonstrated that elites can

[4] See also work by Munger (2017), as described in Section 6.

influence how people think and even talk about political issues (Chong & Druckman 2007; Schaffner & Sellers 2009). And a number of scholars have found that individuals exposed to uncivil elite discourse are more likely to be uncivil in their own discussions about politics (Cappella & Jamieson 1997; Gervais 2014, 2015; Mutz 2006).

At the same time, there is reason to think that elite influence may be limited in the particular realm related to expressions of prejudice. In her classic book *The Race Card*, Mendelberg (2001) finds that the public actually helps to enforce norms regarding expressions of prejudice by penalizing elites who use explicitly racist campaign appeals. Yet, there have been several violations of the "norm of racial equality" in recent years, with the most notable example coming in the form of Donald Trump's presidential campaign. Trump's entry into the presidential race itself included the aforementioned rant targeting Mexicans that was widely criticized as offensive and beyond the pale of normal political discourse, even by many of his fellow Republicans. This speech was only a sign of what was to come, however, as Trump went on to frequently violate norms of civil discourse, particularly when it came to comments relating to various identity groups (Gross & Johnson 2016). Yet, contrary to the expectations laid out by Mendelberg (2001), these remarks (and the subsequent criticism) did not derail his campaign. Notably, the fact that Trump did not suffer a significant penalty for his many prejudiced remarks is consistent with more recent experimental evidence which shows that the public no longer penalizes elite expressions of explicit prejudice in the same way that it once did (Valentino, Neuner & Vandenbroek 2018).

One culprit for these shifting findings regarding the enforcement of norms may be the rise of negative partisanship in contemporary American politics (Iyengar, Sood & Lelkes 2012). Partisans have developed increasingly negative emotions about the opposite party over the course of the past two decades, leading to a process of affective polarization. This affective polarization may be driven by the fact that the public's partisan identities increasingly overlap with their social identities, such as race, ethnicity, and religion (Mason 2016). As Mason and Wronski (2018) note, "the convergence of social identities along partisan lines makes in-party preference more powerful and out-party tolerance ever more difficult." A potential consequence of such a process is to make the public particularly susceptible to influence from elite rhetoric (Tajfel & Turner 1979). This happens at least partly because affective polarization leads people to experience more emotions of anger against the opposing party (Huddy, Mason & Aarøe, 2015; Mason 2016). This increased anger tends to lead people to engage in what is called partisan motivated reasoning (Weeks 2015). This means that people are less likely to view rhetoric from members of their own party through a critical lens and will instead be motivated to defend that rhetoric and even be influenced by it.

Motivated reasoning occurs when people assess new information with a goal to "arrive at a particular conclusion" (Kunda 1990). In politics, partisan goals often dominate reasoning (Bullock 2009; Campbell et al. 1960; Druckman & Bolsen 2011; Petersen et al. 2013; Taber & Lodge 2006), leading people to hold incorrect information about the state of the world because such information reinforces their partisan preferences. Partisan motivations generally lead people to be open to statements and views made by their own co-partisans while they reject arguments made by those from the other party (Zaller 1992).

It is easy to see how partisan motivated reasoning may lead individuals to accept, and ultimately express, more prejudice. A person who otherwise might be reluctant to express or tolerate prejudicial viewpoints may feel significantly better about doing so if it helps them achieve partisan motivated goals. For example, a sexist Republican may generally mask the extent to which they agree with prejudiced statements in order to maintain a positive self-image. However, if they are asked to assess Donald Trump's use of prejudiced language, then their calculation changes. There may still be a desire to maintain a positive self-image by expressing displeasure with such statements, but there is also a countervailing desire not to be critical of the party's presidential nominee. Put another way, expressions of prejudice are easier to justify when they allow one to avoid the cognitive dissonance that would come from being critical of something said by a prominent politician in a person's preferred political party.

1.4 Expectations

It is clear that people tend to suppress (to varying extents) how much prejudice they express externally. There are many reasons for this suppression, but I argue that the key factor to understand in relation to the Trump effect has to do with perceived norms. Specifically, people generally believe that societal norms preclude more explicit expressions of prejudice and most people therefore suppress such expressions in order to conform with these norms. This happens because people care about what others think of them but also because they care about how they view themselves. However, when a politician they like violates these norms, they may take this as a signal that the norms are less clear and uniformly endorsed than they previously thought. If people perceive norms to be potentially more permissive, then they will be less motivated to suppress their own prejudices.

On one hand, it is possible that people may take elite expressions of prejudice as influential signals about norms even when those elites are members of the opposite party. After all, one need not support Trump or the Republican Party to take Trump's rhetoric as a signal that it is permissible to say more prejudiced things publicly without suffering social sanctions.

On the other hand, it is far more likely the case that this effect will be conditioned by partisanship. After all, people tend to be receptive to influence from political leaders from their own party, but they tend to reject rhetoric from politicians from the opposite party (Zaller 1992). Indeed, as I note in Section 1.6, there is evidence that Democrats have reacted to Trump by actually becoming significantly less prejudiced on survey items. Thus, it seems likely that even prejudiced Democrats will be unaffected by Trump's rhetoric, since they may simply reject his statements as irrelevant when it comes to their understanding of norms. Or, their dislike of Trump may even cause them to suppress their own prejudices even further in order to avoid making or endorsing statements that have become central to Trump's brand.

1.5 Evidence for the Trump Effect

A number of studies released in the past few years have purported to show evidence of a Trump effect. As I noted earlier, during the 2016 campaign Costello (2016) presented data from a survey of educators who reported that they felt as though students were engaging in more name-calling toward groups that Trump had targeted during the campaign. Of course, a study like this is merely suggestive; after all, teachers' own perceptions may have been influenced by Trump's campaign, causing them to notice more prejudice in their classrooms or to believe that expressions of prejudice had increased when they had not.

Other observational studies have also found associations between Trump's presence on the national political stage and an increase in expressed prejudice. For example, Edwards and Rushin (2018) use a time series analysis of the FBI's Uniform Crime Report data to show that hate crimes increased significantly during the last three months of 2016, coinciding with Trump's election as president. The increase in the incidence in hate crimes was found especially in counties that voted strongly for Trump in 2016.

The increase in hate crimes that Edwards and Rushin (2018) attribute to Trump's election amount to 410 additional hate crimes per quarter, nationally. This highlights the fact that hate crimes are a particularly rare and extreme expression of prejudice. It also raises the question of whether Trump is simply emboldening a very small share of people to commit extreme acts of prejudice or whether the Trump effect is actually more widespread and extends to everyday expressions of prejudice.

Indeed, some evidence suggests that people are actually expressing less prejudice since Trump's election. For example, Sides, Tesler, and Vavreck (2018) show that Democrats answered questions about racial attitudes and evaluations of immigrants and Muslims in less xenophobic ways after Trump's rise as a presidential candidate (more on this in Section 1.6). Hopkins and Washington (2020) use a panel survey to track anti-black and anti-Hispanic prejudice among a representative sample of white Americans from 2008 to 2018. The survey asked respondents to rate blacks, Hispanics, and whites on scales relating to work ethic (hard working vs. lazy) and trustworthiness (trustworthy vs. untrustworthy). The authors find a significant, though modest, decline in anti-black prejudice on these items after the 2016 election (compared to 2012), with both Democrats and Republicans registering lower levels of prejudice. On anti-Hispanic prejudice, they also find a significant decrease among Democrats, though a slight increase among Republicans. Overall, however, the conclusion from this work is that prejudice (as recorded by these survey items) has declined since Trump's emergence onto the political scene.

Importantly, the studies described thus far rely on observational data to make inferences about how Trump's emergence has affected expressions of prejudice. This research is instructive in providing real-world indicators of how expressions of prejudice have changed since Trump's campaign for president. However, the limitation of relying on observational data is the inability to trace these changes directly to Trump's rhetoric.

Newman et al. (2019) do take an experimental approach to study whether people feel emboldened by Trump's rhetoric to act on their prejudice toward Latinos. In a study of participants recruited on Mechanical Turk, the authors test whether exposing subjects to Trump's offensive statement about Mexicans makes subjects more likely to sanction prejudicial behavior in a subsequent vignette. The findings are summarized as follows:

> Exposure to Trump's racially inflammatory speech caused individuals in our study to bring their prejudice to bear on perceptions of the norm environment toward Latinos, as well as in their behavior. What is most striking about our findings is that the emboldening effect of Trump's rhetoric is the most pronounced when other elites in the political system tacitly condone such speech.

Notably, the results show that simply mentioning Trump's name (even without his prejudiced quotation) appears to give subjects more license to express their prejudice and that having other politicians condemn the remarks does not reduce the effects.

Overall, Newman et al. (2019) provide the strongest test to date of the Trump effect. Nevertheless, there are some limitations of this analysis. The most significant is that the outcome variable captures how subjects judge the actions of somebody else, not the extent to which they themselves express prejudice. Additionally, the study only tested whether Trump's rhetoric increased expressions of prejudice toward Latinos, not toward other targets of Trump's remarks (e.g. Muslims, women, etc.).

1.6 The Countervailing Trump Backlash

While my focus in this manuscript is on the effect Trump has had in making some people feel more free to express their prejudice, it is important to note that, in the aggregate, prejudice appears to be on the decline among Americans. In 2019, Matthew Yglesias wrote about the existence of a "Great Awokening," particularly among white Democrats (Yglesias 2019). On many measures of racial attitudes that are tracked by surveys over time, white Democrats have increasingly provided responses that indicate a greater acknowledgement of racism and more favorable views toward people of color.

Of course, it is unclear whether the increasingly anti-racist and anti-xenophobic attitudes expressed by white Democrats are necessarily a reaction to Trump himself. Indeed, to some extent, there was already a trend in motion before Trump's candidacy. For example, the Cooperative Congressional Election Study (CCES) survey includes an item asking respondents whether they agree or disagree that "generations of slavery and discrimination have created conditions that make it difficult for blacks to work their way out of the lower class." In 2010, 48 percent of white Democrats agreed with the statement; four years later, in 2014, that figure had increased to 54 percent. A similar pattern can be found on other surveys tracking other items; the extent to which white Democrats were acknowledging racism and expressing more positive views toward people of color was gradually increasing even before Trump's rise.

But it also seems clear that Trump has accelerated this trend. Returning to the same item referenced in the previous paragraph, by 2018 72 percent of white Democrats agreed that slavery and discrimination had made things difficult for blacks. That amounts to an 18 percentage point increase over views from just four years earlier. By contrast, views among white Republicans on this item did not change at all during the same period: 74 percent of white Republicans disagreed with the statement in 2010, and 74 percent of white Republicans still disagreed with it in 2018. Indeed, Sides et al. (2018) show that a similar pattern holds across a variety of different items asking for attitudes toward

African Americans, immigrants, and Muslims (p. 213). This pattern is also consistent with the findings from research by Hopkins and Washington (2020) discussed in the previous section using panel data where the same respondents were interviewed over time.

Ultimately, then, it seems that Trump may be influencing prejudice in multiple ways. On one hand, some Americans, mainly Democrats, appear to recoil at Trump's explicit attacks on women and people of color, leading them to take a stronger view against racism and xenophobia as a result. While a "great awokening" was already in motion prior to Trump's candidacy, his presence seemingly accelerated the shift in views among white Democrats. On the other hand, more-prejudiced Republicans may be reacting in the opposite direction – not necessarily by becoming still more prejudiced but by feeling more free to express their prejudice to others. While this study explores the latter process – the extent to which Trump's rhetoric leads some people to express their prejudice more than they would otherwise – it is important not to lose sight of the fact that Trump's rhetoric is also leading many whites to acknowledge and condemn racism and xenophobia more than they have in the past. As Sides et al. (2018) aptly note, Trump has "accelerated partisan polarization over the same identity-inflected issues that helped make the 2016 election so divisive" (p. 212).

1.7 How I Test for the Trump Effect

Following Newman et al. (2019), I rely largely (though not entirely) on survey experiments to study the Trump effect. The benefit of this approach is the ability to make stronger claims about causality – that is, does exposure to Trump's rhetoric actually cause people to react by becoming more tolerant of expressions of prejudice and more willing to express prejudice themselves? Some of the experiments specifically use quotations from Trump, while others use a situation involving a hypothetical politician. This is intentional, as it allows me to understand whether the effects are limited to Trump or are likely to manifest when other politicians – including Democrats – violate norms regarding expressions of prejudice.

In some experiments, my dependent variable is the extent to which people are willing to endorse anti-prejudice norms. In other experiments, I actually test whether people are likely to express prejudice themselves when given an open platform for doing so. By testing how rhetoric affects both the endorsement of anti-prejudice norms as well as expressions of actual prejudice, I am able to more directly test not only how people react to elite expressions of rhetoric but also whether those reactions are likely the result of shifting perceptions of norms.

My experiments also focus on treatments aimed at a variety of different kinds of prejudice, including offensive statements targeting blacks, Latinos, Muslims, and women. Since the norms regarding some groups tend to be more clear than they are for others (Kalkan, Layman & Uslaner 2009), focusing on a range of different targets provides a more complete picture of the scope of the problem.

In addition to the experiments, I also use a panel survey to examine how expressions of prejudice were affected by Trump's electoral victory in November 2016. While the panel data is more suggestive, it is still consistent with other studies suggesting that Trump's victory was, itself, a signal about norms regarding expressions of prejudice (Crandall, Miller & White, 2018). The panel survey shows that the same group of Trump supporters expressed more prejudice after Trump's election than they had before it. Thus, these results help to bolster the patterns found in the experiments.

An important point about these data sources is that most of them are from surveys that are designed to be nationally representative. In this way, the findings from these experiments and from the panel survey can be generalized to the population of American adults. This improves on many of the existing experiments related to the Trump effect, which rely largely on convenience samples that are not designed to be nationally representative.

Overall, the findings from these studies are striking. In Section 2, I show that, in surveys fielded just a few months apart, people expressed more sexism and anti-immigrant sentiment after Trump's victory than they had before. In Section 3, I describe how Americans express less discomfort with sexist statements when they are attributed to Trump compared to when they are attributed to a hypothetical acquaintance. And in Section 4, I show that respondents are more likely to write offensive things about Mexicans after being exposed to Trump's prejudiced quote targeting that group.

But the effects are not limited to Trump. In the last two experiments, presented in Sections 5 and 6, I find that even exposure to a prejudiced quote from an unnamed politician can significantly reduce the extent to which people are willing to endorse norms against the expression of prejudice. And, notably, these effects often happen regardless of the individual's partisanship. That is, people appear to take signals about norms even from politicians from the opposing party.

Of course, no single experiment or finding presented here can be taken as conclusive proof that Trump's prejudiced rhetoric alters peoples' views of the norms and causes some of them to express more prejudice as a result. But together, the results from these four experiments, conducted over the span of three years, tell a compelling and chilling story about how Trump has affected the way that Americans perceive norms to be more permissive than they may have otherwise thought. And these shifting perceptions of norms open the door to allowing many Americans to express more of their own prejudices. In short, the Trump effect is real, and the consequences are troubling.

2 Trump's Victory and Increased Agreement with Prejudiced Statements

As noted earlier, there are strong norms against the expression of explicit prejudice (Dovidio & Gaertner 1986; Rokeach & Ball-Rokeach 1989). These norms serve to increase the suppression of prejudice even among those who hold prejudicial views. However, when people receive signals about the shifting of norms, or when norms are ambiguous, there are increased justifications to express prejudice (Blanchard et al. 1994, 1991; Paluck 2009; Zitek & Hebl 2007). One salient signal about social norms relates to the perceived prevalence of prejudice among one's peers. After all, people may feel more justified to express prejudiced viewpoints when they believe that many other people like themselves share those viewpoints. Social psychology experiments have found consistent support for this expectation – people tend to express lower levels of prejudice when they are made to think that others are not prejudiced, and they express more prejudice when they believe the opposite is true (Blanchard et al. 1994, 1991; Zitek & Hebl 2007).

Based on this existing body of work, it is reasonable to expect that the 2016 presidential election may have served as a signal to many individuals about the prevalence of sexist and xenophobic attitudes among the American public. After all, Trump frequently made high-profile sexist and xenophobic comments during the campaign. The Clinton campaign focused considerable attention on Trump's prejudiced remarks and actions in an attempt to dissuade voters from supporting him. Furthermore, in late October 2016, when I was first interviewing respondents for this study, Trump was widely expected to lose the election. In fact, a poll conducted by CNN two weeks before the election showed that just 27 percent of Americans thought he would win.[5] In such a climate, prejudiced Trump supporters may have felt that their views were not widely shared and thus felt more motivated to suppress their prejudice.

And then Trump won the election, a victory that surprised most Americans and likely shifted people's perceptions about the extent to which the prejudices that Trump verbalized on the campaign trail were widely held. Indeed, there is evidence that the election did play such a role. Crandall et al. (2018) interviewed a convenience sample of 388 individuals recruited via Amazon's Mechanical Turk platform before and after the 2016 election. The researchers found that

[5] See www.cnn.com/2016/10/25/politics/hillary-clinton-2016-election-poll/index.html.

subjects perceived a higher level of tolerance for prejudicial viewpoints after the election than they had before and that this was largely limited to the groups that Trump had targeted during the campaign. As Crandall et al. (2018) note, "It was most likely the election itself – the public endorsement of Trump by the American people – that changed perceptions."

2.1 Panel Survey

Did Trump's election serve as a justification for people to reduce the extent to which they suppressed their prejudice? To answer this question, I use data from a nationally representative panel survey of 1,000 American adults interviewed in two waves. The first wave of the survey was conducted October 25–31, 2016, just before the election. The second wave was fielded March 1–20, 2017, about six weeks after Trump was inaugurated.[6] Respondents were recruited and interviewed by the survey firm YouGov. They completed the self-administered questionnaire online and were matched to a target sample to ensure that they were representative of the American adult population.

The panel survey is a particularly useful way to test for whether people changed how much prejudice they expressed on surveys because reinterviewing the same set of respondents reduces concerns that might arise from comparing different samples over time. With the panel approach, the same individuals are responding to the same questions at different points of time, meaning that any change I detect cannot be attributed to factors like a change in the composition of the sample.

For each of the analyses I present, the main independent variable is time – specifically, I am testing for whether individuals express more prejudice following Trump's election as president. Because we might expect Trump's strongest supporters to be most affected by the impact of his victory, I also separate the analyses that follow based on how people felt about Trump when they were interviewed in wave 1.

The first dependent variable for the analysis is each respondent's average agreement with four items from the hostile sexism battery developed by Glick and Fiske (1996). Hostile sexism – simply defined as prejudice and hostility toward women – plays a prevalent role in modern American society. Even in recent surveys, many Americans are willing to agree to statements that suggest a resentment toward women who push for gender equality. For example, in the 2016 wave of this survey, nearly one in four Americans of both sexes agreed with the statement that "women seek to gain power by getting control over

[6] A third wave was in the field from July 17 to August 3, 2018; however, to preserve sample size and combat attrition bias, I only analyze the first two waves here.

men," while over 30 percent expressed agreement that "when women lose to men in a fair competition, they typically complain about being discriminated against." These items coincide with the brand of sexism that Donald Trump appealed to when calling Clinton a "nasty woman" or complaining about her use of the "woman card." Schaffner, MacWilliams, and Nteta (2018) find that individuals with the highest levels of hostile sexism voted for Trump by 20–30 points more than the least sexist people, even when controlling for racial attitudes, economic indicators, demographics, partisanship, and ideology. Other studies have demonstrated a similar role for sexism in predicting support for Trump, even during the primaries (Valentino, Wayne & Oceno 2018).

In each wave of the survey, respondents were asked to register the extent to which they agreed or disagreed with the following hostile sexism items:

- Many women are actually seeking special favors, such as hiring policies that favor them over men, under the guise of asking for "equality."
- Women are too easily offended.
- Women seek to gain power by getting control over men.
- When women lose to men in a fair competition, they typically complain about being discriminated against.

Responses were given on a five-point scale ranging from "disagree strongly" (1) to "agree strongly" (5), with strong agreement indicating higher levels of hostile sexism. Here, I examine the average percentage of the time that respondents agreed with the four statements.

A second dependent variable focuses on responses to a question about illegal immigrants, a group frequently targeted by Trump both during the campaign and since his election. Specifically, the item asked respondents to indicate the extent to which they agreed with the following statement: "Illegal immigrants pose a threat to public safety." This statement captures prejudice toward immigrants, particularly by linking them to crime and violence. Thus, some Americans may feel that agreeing (especially strongly agreeing) with this statement might reveal prejudice. In the first wave of the survey (prior to Trump's victory), just 14 percent strongly agreed with the statement and another 20 percent somewhat agreed.

As noted, I expect that Trump's election will increase agreement with these statements, particularly among those who have a very favorable opinion of him. Thus, I examine the change in responses according to how a respondent rated Trump in the first wave of the survey. Specifically, I divide respondents into three groups: (1) those that said they had a very favorable view of Trump (N = 202); (2) those with a somewhat favorable or somewhat unfavorable view of Trump (N = 236); and (3) those who rated Trump very unfavorably (N = 560).

2.2 Results

Figure 1 shows the average percentage of the time that each group agreed with the four hostile sexism statements. The vertical bars in the figure represent 84 percent confidence intervals. I use 84 percent confidence intervals to make it easier for the reader to detect statistically significant differences. When the 84 percent confidence intervals for a pair of estimates do not overlap, that means we can be 95 percent confident that the two values are different among the population of American adults (Julious 2004).

Even in wave 1, Trump supporters were much more likely to agree with hostile sexism statements than were other respondents. On average, people who rated Trump very favorably in October 2016 agreed with hostile sexism statements about 44 percent of the time. By comparison, those who had a very unfavorable view of him agreed with those statements just 15 percent of the time.

But the election appeared to embolden Trump's strongest supporters even further. Indeed, two months after Trump's inauguration, respondents who had rated Trump very favorably in October agreed with the same hostile sexism statements about 55 percent of the time – an increase of 11 percentage points

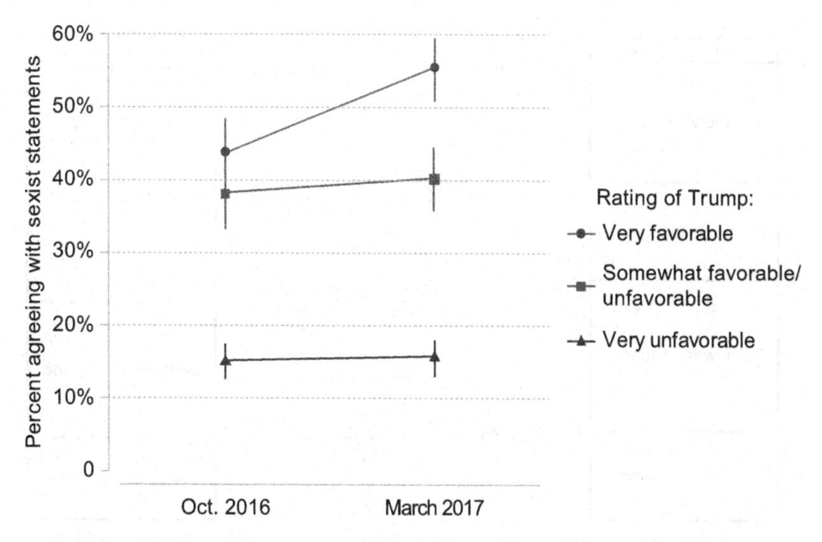

Figure 1 Agreement with hostile sexism statements by Trump support, October 2016 to March 2017

Note: Vertical lines represent 84 percent confidence intervals.

over wave 1 (p = .01). By contrast, for respondents who were agnostic or antagonistic toward Trump, there was no statistically significant or substantively meaningful change in agreement with sexist statements after the election.

Recall that the justification/suppression model of prejudice would lead us to expect that people who were suppressing prejudice before the election may have felt justification to reduce that suppression after Trump's victory. This theory can help to inform where we might most expect to observe change in the questions that comprise the hostile sexism battery. For example, an individual who is prejudiced toward women would generally express agreement (or strong agreement) with the four statements they answered from the hostile sexism battery. However, in suppressing such a response, that individual might instead select the neutral value on the scale. It is less likely that the act of suppression would move the individual all the way toward expressing disagreement with the statement. Thus, we might expect to find that the increased sexism expressed after the election largely came from people who gave neutral responses to the hostile sexism questions before the election.

Figure 2 provides more detail on how movement occurred between waves 1 and 2 on the hostile sexism items. The left-hand side of the plot shows the proportion at each level of agreement with the four hostile sexism items in wave 1, while the right-hand side shows the same for wave 2. The shaded areas between these show the flow of respondents from each category in wave 1. For example, 5 percent of respondents averaged a "strongly agree" response to the

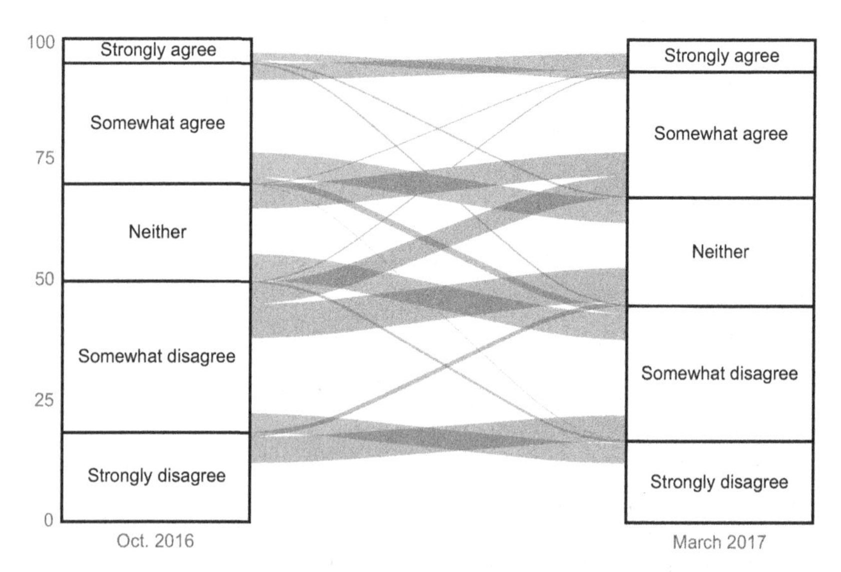

Figure 2 Movement between categories on hostile sexism items, October 2016 to March 2017

sexism items in wave 1; in wave 2, 7 percent averaged strong agreement with those statements. Most of the additional "strongly agree" respondents in wave 2 came from those who somewhat agreed in wave 1. In fact, 3 percent of the sample averaged a "somewhat agree" response in wave 1 but moved into the "strongly agree" group in wave 2.

The percentage of respondents who averaged a "somewhat agree" response to the hostile sexism items also slightly increased from 22 percent to 26 percent between waves 1 and 2. Much of this net increase was due to respondents who averaged a "neither agree nor disagree" or "somewhat disagree" response to the hostile sexism statements in wave 1. 5 percent of respondents moved from "neither" to "somewhat agree" between waves 1 and 2 and another 4 percent moved from "somewhat disagree" to "somewhat agree." The latter movement is especially interesting, since only 1 percent moved in the opposite direction – from "somewhat agree" to "somewhat disagree" – during the same period. Overall, 26 percent of respondents moved in a more sexist direction between waves 1 and 2, while just 19 percent gave responses that were less sexist.

I now turn to examining whether panelists shifted their responses to the item about illegal immigrants being a threat to public safety. Figure 3 shows the percentage of each group who strongly agreed with the statement that "illegal immigrants pose a threat to public safety" in each wave. We see a very similar pattern to that shown for the hostile sexism items in Figure 1. About 38 percent

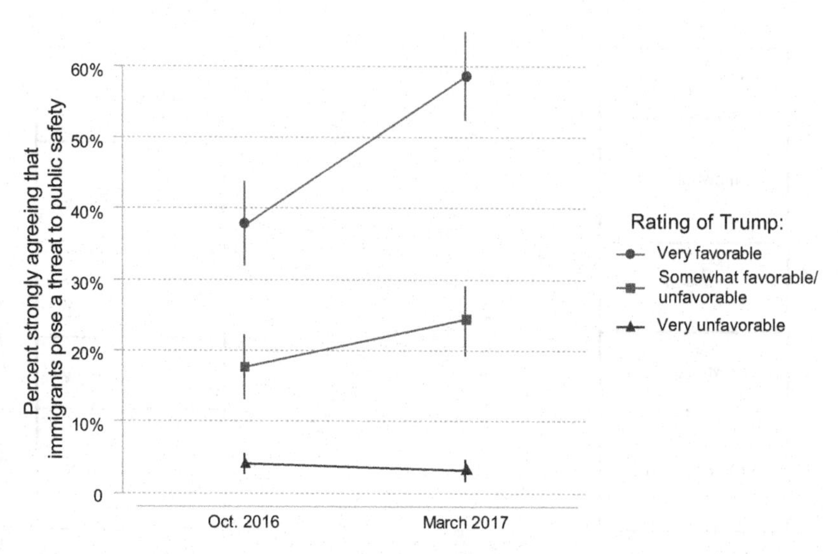

Figure 3 Agreement that immigrants are a threat to public safety by Trump support, October 2016 to March 2017

Note: Vertical lines represent 84 percent confidence intervals.

of Trump's strongest supporters strongly agreed with that statement before the election, but that increased to 59 percent in March 2017. The 21-point increase is statistically significant (p = .001) and even larger than the shift we saw among Trump supporters on the hostile sexism items.

Among the other two groups, we do not see similar change. Those who had middling views of Trump in wave 1 (those who rated him somewhat favorably or somewhat unfavorably) did see a modest increase in strong agreement, but it was not statistically significant. Trump's strongest opponents were already very unlikely to strongly agree with the statement about immigrants before the election (4 percent), and little changed for that group after the election (3 percent).

Figure 4 shows the movement in respondents between categories of agreement from wave 1 to wave 2. Note that there is a 39 percent increase in the proportion of respondents who "strongly agree" with the statement in wave 2 compared to wave 1. Specifically, while 14 percent "strongly agreed" in October 2016, 20 percent did the same just five months later. This increase largely comes from those who were in the "somewhat agree" category in wave 1. Indeed, 6 percent of panelists moved from "somewhat agree" to "strongly agree" between waves 1 and 2. Overall, 26 percent of respondents gave a more anti-immigrant response in wave 2 than they had in wave 1, while just 20 percent moved in the opposite direction.

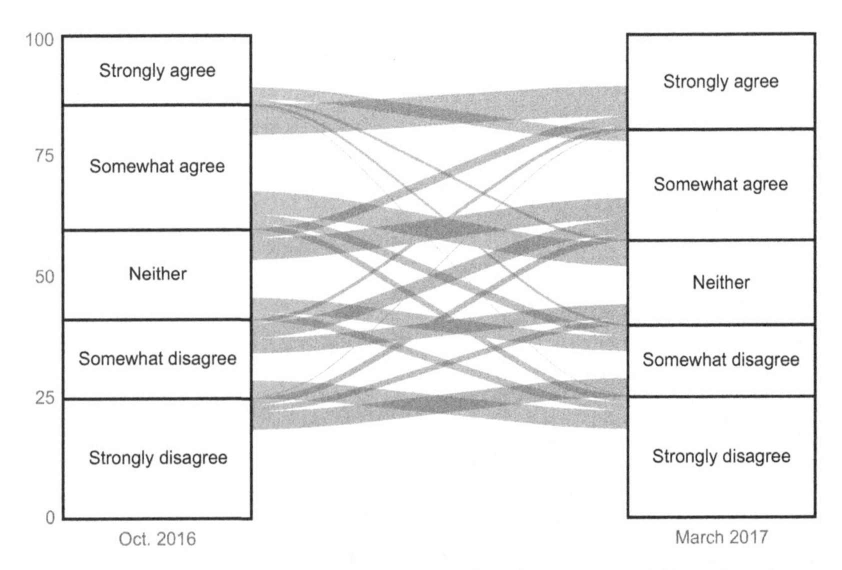

Figure 4 Movement between categories on immigrants as public safety threat statement, October 2016 to March 2017

2.3 Summary

Overall, the patterns from the panel survey provide some tenuous support for the "Trump effect" thesis. At least when it comes to statements about women and illegal immigrants, Trump voters were more likely to agree with prejudiced statements a few months after Trump's victory than they had been during the weeks before the election. This suggests that Trump's victory may have served as a signal about norms to some people who had previously done more to hide their prejudice. Indeed, recall that Crandall et al. (2018) found that people reported an increase in the perceived acceptability of expressing prejudice after Trump's victory. The findings from this panel survey suggest that some shifted their own expressions of prejudice as a result.

However, the panel data is a limited way to study this phenomenon. Ideally, the survey would have included additional measures of prejudice focusing on other groups so that we could examine how widespread this phenomenon was. Additionally, it is impossible to know for sure whether it was Trump's victory that led to more agreement with prejudiced statements rather than other events that occurred during the intervening five-month period. Thus, the data presented in this section is best thought of as descriptive and suggestive in nature. To gain a better test of whether Trump's rhetoric is actually causing the changes we see here, an experimental approach is needed. Thus, in the following sections I present results from a series of four experiments I conducted between 2016 and 2019.

3 Acceptance of Trump's Sexist Rhetoric

While the main focus of this study is on how Trump's rhetoric affects people's own expressions of prejudice, the first experiment focuses on an intermediary step – the extent to which people express discomfort with prejudiced rhetoric from Trump. As I discussed in Section 1, for many years political scientists expected that people would reject and punish politicians who expressed prejudice explicitly (Mendelberg 2001). But, perhaps due to the increasing affective polarization in the United States, it now appears to be the case that the public will not punish political leaders for explicit expressions of prejudice (Valentino, Neuner & Vandenbroek 2018). In other words, at least when it comes to explicit expressions of racial prejudice, politicians need no longer be concerned that they will suffer an electoral penalty.

My first experiment focuses specifically on the willingness of people to express discomfort with elite expressions of prejudice – in this case, sexism. The 2016 presidential election put sexism at center stage. Trump frequently directed sexist rhetoric at Clinton, accusing her of "playing the woman card" and referring to her as a "nasty woman." Rhetoric relating to gender and sexism became even more central during the final month of the campaign when the *Access Hollywood* tape created controversy about Trump's treatment of women. Indeed, one of Clinton's final advertisements during the campaign featured a litany of Trump's sexist quotations before ending with the argument that these statements made Trump unfit to be president.[7]

The experiment I present in this section focuses on expressed discomfort with sexist statements when they are attributed to Trump rather than to a hypothetical acquaintance. The experiment allows me to test more directly the role of partisan motivated reasoning in how individuals react to elite expressions of prejudice. Notably, I do find that partisan motivations appear to make sexist Trump supporters more accepting of sexist rhetoric when it comes from Trump rather than a hypothetical acquaintance. By contrast, sexist Clinton supporters express more discomfort with the sexist comments when they come from Trump rather than from an acquaintance.

3.1 Experimental Design

This experiment was fielded on a module to the 2016 Cooperative Congressional Election Study (CCES). The experiment appeared on the pre-election questionnaire and was administered to 1,000 respondents who were interviewed between September 28 and November 6. The CCES is an NSF-funded survey about politics that is fielded each year. Extensive detail about the methodology of the CCES survey can be found in the guide to the CCES.[8] Like the survey described in the previous section, the CCES is also fielded by YouGov and conducted online with a set of respondents who are selected to be representative of American adults on a variety of demographic and political factors.

The experiment was designed to ask respondents about the types of comments Donald Trump made about women in the past. In the control condition, respondents were given the following hypothetical scenario:

> Imagine that during a conversation, a male acquaintance referred to one woman as "a dog" and then later in the same conversation referred to his wife as a "beautiful piece of ass."

Respondents were then asked how these comments would make them feel on a five-point scale ranging from "very uncomfortable" to "very comfortable." In the treatment condition, respondents were told the following:

[7] The advertisement, "What he believes," was released by the Clinton campaign on November 1, 2016: see www.youtube.com/watch?v=Oy8HRdlLGCQ.

[8] See https://doi.org/10.7910/DVN/GDF6Z0.

> During the past year, Donald Trump publicly referred to one woman as "a dog" and referred to his wife as a "beautiful piece of ass."

Respondents were then asked how the statements made them feel and were given the same five-point scale for their responses. For the analysis, I examine the effect of the treatment on the percentage of respondents who reported that they were very or somewhat uncomfortable with the statements.

One thing to note about this experiment is the differing context of the two quotations beyond simply who they are being attributed to. For example, in the acquaintance version, the sexist remarks were said during the course of a single conversation in a private setting. In the Trump condition, the statements happen over a longer time span and in public. Nevertheless, as I will show, it is likely the case that respondents are largely responding to the attribution to Trump.

If motivated reasoning provides a justification for people to tolerate more prejudice, then we should find that Trump supporters in the treatment condition are more comfortable with the statements than those in the control condition. This would occur because Republicans' partisan motives provide a justification for undermining their motivations to hide their prejudice. For Clinton supporters, either their discomfort with these statements should not differ across the treatment and control conditions or they may even express more discomfort with the statements in the Trump condition since any partisan motives would reinforce their suppression motives.

To divide respondents into Trump and Clinton supporters, I use a question about vote intention from the preelection survey. This question was asked before respondents encountered the experiment. However, for a small number of respondents, I use their stated vote choice (or vote preference) on the postelection wave of the survey (since some respondents did not reveal their vote preference in the preelection wave). I do this to maximize the power for my experimental test. Nevertheless, the findings presented are consistent regardless of whether I only use the preelection vote choice question or if I use both the pre- and postelection vote choice questions. Additionally, the findings are also consistent if I use party identification rather than vote choice. The analysis that follows includes 502 Clinton backers and 342 Trump supporters.

3.2 Results

Figure 5 shows the percentage expressing discomfort with the statements based on the vote choice of the respondent and the version of the question that they received. The vertical lines represent 84 percent confidence intervals for the estimates – this means that when the confidence intervals do not overlap we can be 95 percent confident that the differences in the estimates are

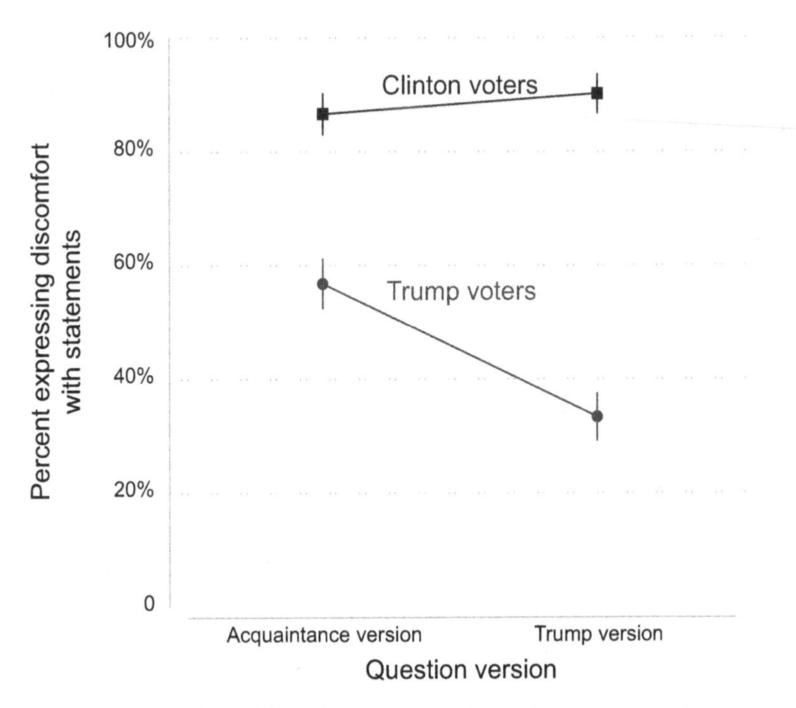

Figure 5 Discomfort with sexist statements depending on source, by vote preference

Note: Vertical lines represent 84 percent confidence intervals.

statistically significant. Note that, even in the acquaintance version, Trump supporters were about 30 percentage points less likely to express discomfort with the remarks compared to Clinton supporters (57 percent of Trump supporters expressed discomfort compared to 87 percent of Clinton voters). This is not particularly surprising since Trump supporters registered higher levels of sexism than Clinton voters (Schaffner et al. 2018; Valentino, Wayne & Oceno 2018).

The key point of interest is the comparison of responses for those in the acquaintance version with those in the version where Trump was tied to the statements. Here we see clear evidence that partisan-motivated reasoning led Trump supporters to express more tolerance for sexist rhetoric. In particular, while 57 percent of Trump voters were uncomfortable with the statements when they were uttered by an acquaintance, that figure dropped to just 33 percent when those statements were attributed to Trump. This amounts to a 21 percentage point drop in discomfort when partisan motivations are introduced ($p < .001$). By comparison, there is virtually no difference in the percentage of Clinton supporters expressing discomfort in either condition – 87 percent said they were uncomfortable with the remarks when they were attributed to an acquaintance while 90 percent were uncomfortable when they came from Trump.

However, grouping the "very uncomfortable" and "somewhat uncomfortable" response categories together masks some movement among Clinton supporters. Table 1 shows more detail about the distribution of responses in the acquaintance and Trump versions. Among Clinton backers, there is a shift away from the "somewhat uncomfortable" category ($p = .025$) and an increase in the percentage saying that the statements make them "very uncomfortable" ($p = .011$). Overall, Democrats were even more willing to indicate that the statements made them "very uncomfortable" (rather than "somewhat uncomfortable") when they came from Trump.

However, most interesting is the shift among Republicans. There is a large 21- point drop in the percentage of respondents selecting "very uncomfortable" when the statements are attributed to Trump ($p < .001$) and a large 14-percentage point increase in those saying that the statements make them "neither uncomfortable nor comfortable" ($p = .003$). And while very few respondents ever say that the statements make them feel comfortable, there is a statistically significant increase in the propensity of choosing the comfortable categories when the quotes are attributed to Trump. In fact, Trump supporters are three times more likely to say that the statements make them feel somewhat or very comfortable when they are attributed to Trump rather than to an acquaintance (13 percent versus 4 percent, respectively; $p < .001$).

3.3 The Role of Sexism

Given that the remarks in this experiment target women, we might expect that a respondent's level of hostile sexism would moderate the effects of the

Table 1 Distribution of responses in acquaintance and Trump conditions by vote preference

	Clinton voters		**Trump voters**	
	Acquaintance	**Trump**	**Acquaintance**	**Trump**
Very uncomfortable	64%	76%	34%	13%
Somewhat uncomfortable	23%	14%	23%	20%
Neither	9%	6%	40%	54%
Somewhat comfortable	3%	1%	2%	6%
Very comfortable	2%	3%	2%	7%

treatment.[9] Figure 6 shows the treatment effects from the experiment broken down by both candidate support and how the respondent scored on four hostile sexism items. Specifically, the CCES questionnaire included the same four items described in the previous section, and I divided respondents based on whether they were above or below the mean score for these items.[10]

The patterns displayed in Figure 6 are striking. Notably, the treatment mostly only affects respondents who scored above the mean on the hostile sexism items, but it affects sexist Trump supporters in the opposite way to how it affects sexist Clinton backers. In the acquaintance condition, sexist Clinton supporters were about as likely to say that the statements made them feel as uncomfortable as were both sexist and nonsexist Trump backers. However, when the quotations were attributed to Trump, these evaluations shifted. In particular, high-sexism Trump voters became about 28 percentage points less likely to say the statements made them uncomfortable when they were connected to Trump. By contrast, high-sexism Clinton supporters were about 24 percentage points *more* likely to say the statements made them feel uncomfortable when they came from

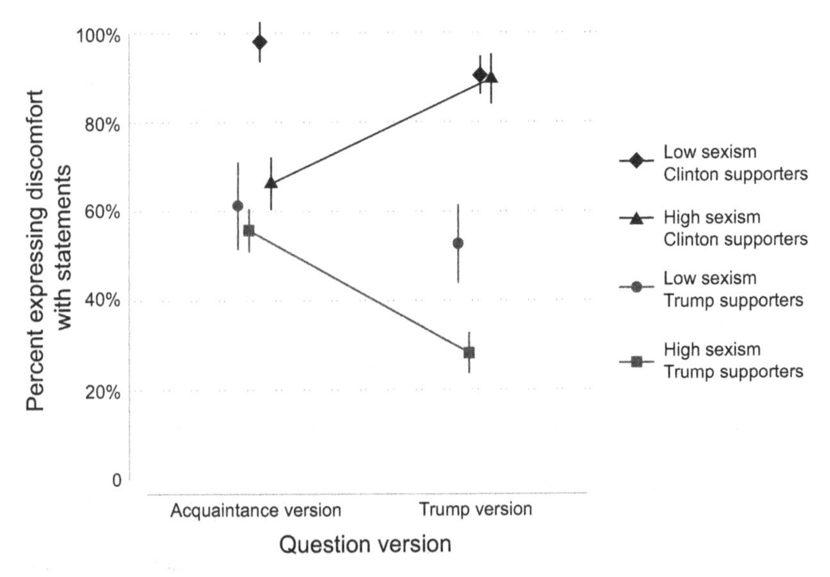

Figure 6 Treatment effects of attributing statements to Trump conditional on respondent's vote preference and gender

Note: Vertical lines represent 84 percent confidence intervals.

[9] We might also expect sex to matter, but research on sexism shows that many women hold fairly sexist attitudes themselves (Becker 2010), meaning that they may actually respond to the treatment in a similar fashion as their male counterparts. In the online supplementary materials, I show that the treatment effects are consistent for both men and women.

[10] These sexism items were asked much earlier in the questionnaire.

Trump. At the same time, the Trump treatment did not have a statistically significant effect on how low-sexism respondents evaluated the statements, regardless of which candidate they supported.

There is another way of looking at the patterns in Figure 6, one that is instructive. Specifically, absent the connection to Trump, there was a sizable gap in how low- versus high-sexism Clinton supporters evaluated the statements. This suggests that, absent the partisan cue, sexism was a strong predictor of how Democrats evaluated those quotations. However, once the Trump connection was introduced, this gap disappeared, and more-sexist Clinton backers were just as likely as less-sexist Clinton supporters to say that the quotes made them feel uncomfortable. This indicates that the partisan motivations introduced by connecting the quotations to Trump override the extent to which these individuals might otherwise be willing to tolerate the remarks.

By contrast, the introduction of the Trump connection creates differing levels of discomfort among more- and less-sexist Republicans. This suggests that, for many in-party respondents, the Trump connection may provide license to reveal more tolerance for sexism than sexist Republicans would be willing to express otherwise. Indeed, sexist Trump supporters are twice as likely to say that the sexist quotes make them feel uncomfortable when they are attributed to an acquaintance compared to when they are connected to Trump.

3.4 Summary

The findings from this experiment have provided a second piece of evidence regarding how influential Trump's rhetoric may be. Specifically, the fact that Trump supporters reported that these sexist statements made them less uncomfortable when they were attributed to Trump suggests that Trump's stature as a prominent Republican politician may have created some normative ambiguity regarding the appropriateness of these remarks. Notably, this effect was largely found among the most sexist Trump supporters, whereas Trump backers who scored lower on the hostile sexism scale did not see a statistically significant alteration in how they evaluated the statements when they were connected to Trump.

It is also worth noting how sexist Democrats responded in an opposite manner – they were less uncomfortable with the statements when attributed to an acquaintance, but once those quotes were connected to Trump they expressed just as much discomfort with them as the less-sexist Clinton supporters. This suggests that partisan motivations provide a counterpressure to sexist Clinton backers, causing them to provide anti-sexist responses to the stimulus when it is connected to a politician they dislike. Recall from Section 1 of this Element that a variety of survey measures show a dramatic anti-prejudice shift among white Democrats since Trump's rise on the political scene. The findings from this experiment help us to make sense of this pattern – even sexist Democrats express less tolerance for sexist remarks when those remarks are connected to Trump. In short, partisanship appears to be motivating Democrats to adjust how they think and talk about out-groups (Engelhardt 2018).

Returning to the reaction among Trump supporters, it may be that they expressed less discomfort with these statements merely because they were attributed to a politician whom they trust. And if attributing these statements to Trump made his supporters more comfortable with hearing them, then it may be that it would also make them more likely to express their own sexism as well. In the following section, I more directly test whether Trump's expressions of prejudice do indeed have such an effect.

4 A Direct Test of the Trump Effect

In this section, I shift my focus specifically to the question of whether being exposed to prejudiced statements made by Trump increases the likelihood that people will actually express more prejudice themselves. This is the core claim of the Trump effect – the idea that Trump doesn't necessarily make people more prejudiced but that his rhetoric and presence as a major political figure makes prejudiced people feel more free to express their prejudice to others. As noted earlier, this is a difficult claim to test. After all, we cannot observe what the world would be like if Trump had not run for or ultimately won the presidency. But in this section I present a direct test of the Trump effect in which I randomly exposed some people to Trump's prejudiced rhetoric and then observed whether they were subseqently more willing to write offensive things about out-groups.

As far as I am aware, this is the most direct test yet of whether people express more prejudice when they hear Trump do the same.

4.1 Design

I fielded an experiment in 2016 on a nationally representative sample fielded by YouGov. Like the experiment in the previous section, this one was fielded on the 2016 CCES preelection questionnaire and was administered to 1,186 non-Latino white adult respondents who completed the online survey between September 28 and November 6.[11]

[11] A second experiment was fielded on 656 non-Latino non-Muslim white respondents who were interviewed between November 8 and December 9, 2017, as part of the 2017 CCES. Due to the small sample size, I only discuss this experiment briefly at the end of this section.

The primary aim of the experiment was to test whether respondents who were exposed to Trump's offensive comments about minority groups would themselves express more negative sentiments about those groups. However, it was important to disguise (as much as possible) the point of the experiment in order to minimize demand effects. As a result, exposure to the treatments was embedded in a question that was ostensibly seeking to measure how much attention respondents had paid to the presidential campaign. Specifically, the question asked respondents to identify which candidate made each of a series of statements during the presidential campaign. The preamble for this question read: "Now we will show you several statements made by the presidential candidates during the previous year. Please indicate which candidate you think made these statements."

The control group saw just the following three statements:

1 "Obama has no solutions. Obama has failed the country and its great citizens."
2 "If I want to knock a story off the front page, I just change my hairstyle."
3 "My two secrets to staying healthy: wash your hands all the time. And, if you can't, use Purell or one of the sanitizers. And the other is hot peppers. I eat a lot of hot peppers. I for some reason started doing that in 1992, and I swear by it."

Respondents saw one statement at a time and were asked to indicate whether Hillary Clinton or Donald Trump had made the remark, or if they were not sure. There were two treatment statements. Respondents had a 50 percent chance of seeing each of these treatment statements; this means that about one-fourth of the sample (N = 301) saw no treatment statements; half saw one treatment statement (N = 268 and 277, respectively); and one-quarter saw both treatment statements (N = 317). The treatment quotations were:

4 "Our great African-American president hasn't exactly had a positive impact on the thugs who are so happily and openly destroying Baltimore."
5 "When Mexico sends its people, they're not sending their best. They're sending people that have lots of problems. They're bringing drugs. They're bringing crime. They're rapists. And some, I assume, are good people."

Note that the order in which the quotes were presented was randomized for all respondents. The quotation about Mexicans is probably the most explicitly xenophobic of the two; however, in the first treatment quote, Trump's reference to Obama as "African-American" before referring to "thugs" is making a fairly clear connection to common stereotypes of African Americans as being violent and criminal.

Whether they had heard the quotation before or were simply guessing, most respondents were able to identify Trump as the source of the two treatment quotations. Of respondents, 82 percent indicated that Trump produced the quote about Baltimore, while 91 percent attributed the quote about Mexicans to Trump. However, it is important to note that the experiment does not rest on the assumption that respondents were encountering these quotations for the first time. It is true that the fact that many had already heard these quotes may diminish the experimental effects I am able to detect here, since most respondents were likely "pretreated" to some extent. Yet, the experimental treatment still serves to remind the treated respondents (but not those in the control) about Trump's prejudiced rhetoric, therefore priming that consideration in their minds just before I capture their propensity to write negative and offensive things about the groups Trump was targeting.

On the page following the questions asking respondents to identify the source of the quotations, all individuals were told, "In a few words, please let us know what comes to mind when you think of the following groups." Respondents were shown six groups, and for each there was a small text box in which they could type out their responses. Respondents were asked to write a brief comment about blacks, Mexicans, whites, politicians, the middle class, and millennials.[12] The order in which the groups appeared was randomized. While the target groups of interest for this experiment are blacks and Mexicans (the targets of Trump's offensive comments), the additional groups were included for two reasons. First, the additional groups helped to further disguise the purpose of this question vis-à-vis the experiment. Second, by including these additional groups, I can test for whether Trump's offensive comments actually make respondents speak more negatively about a broader array of groups than were targeted in Trump's remarks. For the analysis that follows, I also analyze comments about millennials for this purpose.[13]

4.2 Coding Respondent Comments

The open-ended responses represent the dependent variable of interest for these experiments; it is here where I expect to find increased expressions of prejudice. However, the challenge is determining the best approach to coding these responses. Because the length of these comments is generally brief, common automated text analysis tools struggle to extract meaningful information from them. Many respondents entered just one word in the boxes, such as

[12] The median response for comments about blacks in the 2016 experiment is just seventeen characters in length.

[13] As I will explain, coding responses required hiring human coders, a costly process. Therefore, I did not code what respondents wrote about all six groups.

"disadvantaged," "entitled," or "misunderstood." Without incorporating the context of the question being answered, it is difficult to automate the categorization of some of these comments as negative or positive in nature. For example, the word "disadvantaged" has a negative tone, but its use here is not suggesting that the individual is saying something negative about blacks. Similarly, the word "entitled" has a positive tone absent context, but in this use the respondent is clearly saying something negative about blacks.

A second option would be to hire research assistants and provide them with clear guidelines regarding what constituted a negative or offensive comment about a particular group. The advantage of this approach would be the ability to clearly define a priori what constitutes offensiveness; however, this can also be a drawback. In particular, what constitutes a negative or offensive comment is naturally a subjective judgment, and ideally any coding scheme should take into account the possibility that there would be some disagreement about these judgments.

Therefore, I chose to use an approach that would solicit ratings from multiple coders drawn from the general population of American adults. Specifically, I recruited Amazon's Mechanical Turk (MTurk) workers to code the open-ended comments respondents wrote about blacks, Mexicans, and millennials. Each worker was shown ten comments, which were randomly assigned from the full list of comments written about one of the groups.[14] The median comment about blacks was rated by seven MTurk workers, and the median comment about Mexicans and millennials was coded by six workers.[15] There was an attention check item provided to each coder to make sure that they were actually reading the comments. Fewer than 2 percent of the MTurk coders failed the attention check; I exclude the ratings from this small number of MTurk coders who did not pass the attention check.

The MTurk workers were told what the question was that people were responding to and were asked to rate each comment on a 100-point scale ranging from "very negative" to "very positive."[16] The MTurkers were not,

---

[14] Each MTurk worker saw ten comments that were all written about the same group (e.g., blacks, Mexicans, millennials, etc.).

[15] After having MTurk workers code the comments about blacks, I was able to increase the efficiency of the process by collapsing identical comments before placing them on MTurk for evaluation.

[16] One might expect that the demographic traits of the MTurk coders would be a factor affecting whether they perceived comments about minority groups to be negative or offensive. To test this, I also collected some limited demographic information about the coders, including ideology, race, gender, and age. I first estimated a fixed effects regression model where the fixed effects were for each unique comment being coded. I then estimated a second model that included the demographics of the coders. Overall, adding the demographic variables to the model typically increased the proportion of the variance in ratings explained by less than 1 percent.

however, informed about the fact that this was part of an experiment and thus had no knowledge of the questions that came before those they were asked to code. Notably, the human coders appeared to be successful in using contextual information to discern the meaning of even brief text. Returning to the earlier example, the comment "entitled" received an average rating of 24 on the scale (clearly negative), while "disadvantaged" received a 43 (close to neutral). After rating each comment on the 100-point scale, MTurk workers were then asked to indicate whether the comment was hateful, offensive, or neither. This question was designed to help identify remarks that were especially negative in a way that MTurk workers would perceive as violating norms of polite discourse. For the analysis that follows, and consistent with Nithyanand, Schaffner, and Gill (2017), I combine the offensive and hateful categories together and refer to such remarks as offensive. The analysis focuses specifically on this measure of offensiveness, but the online supplementary materials shows that the patterns are similar when the negativity scale is used instead.

Figure 7 shows the distribution of comments based on the proportion of coders who rated each as offensive or hateful. The most common classification given to a comment was that it was not offensive or hateful. However, more than one-third of comments written about Mexicans or millennials were rated as offensive by at least one coder, and nearly 60 percent of comments about blacks were classified as offensive by at least one coder. On average, comments about blacks were identified as offensive 29 percent of the time, compared to 20 percent for comments about Mexicans and 22 percent for comments about millennials.

Since having the open-ended responses coded is costly, I limited the coding to the two groups targeted by Trump's quotations (blacks and Mexicans) and

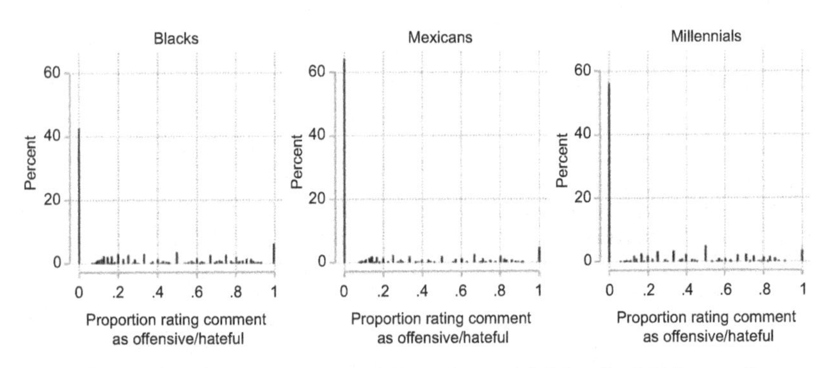

Figure 7 Distribution of values of dependent variables for 2016 experiment
Note: The plots show the distribution of comments based on the proportion of MTurk workers that rated the comment as offensive or hateful.

a third unrelated group (millennials). When survey respondents chose to leave a text box blank, they were automatically coded as not having written anything offensive or hateful. Overall, the MTurk raters exhibited a fairly high level of consistency in how they rated comments. Reliability for the offensiveness categorization was .69 or higher.

4.3 Results

Figure 8 shows the percentage of comments made about each group that were classified as offensive based on whether the respondent was assigned to the control group or one of the treatment conditions. The vertical lines in the plot represent 84 percent confidence intervals; when these intervals do not overlap, it means we can be 95 percent confident that the estimates are different from each other. First, looking at the left-hand plot, we see that exposure to the quotations does not appear to alter the degree to which people made offensive comments about blacks. About 30 percent of whites wrote an offensive comment about blacks on the survey regardless of whether they were exposed to one of Trump's prejudicial statements or not. By looking across the figure at the results for comments about Mexicans and millennials we can also see that whites are much more likely to say something offensive about blacks than they are about Mexicans and millennials. Thus, one reason that Trump's rhetoric may not produce an increase in the rate at which whites write something offensive about blacks is because over one-quarter of whites already feel free to do so even in the control condition.

The middle plot presents the treatment effects on the offensiveness of comments offered about Mexicans. In the control condition, 16 percent of white respondents wrote something about Mexicans that was classified as offensive or hateful. However, when respondents were exposed to Trump's quote about Mexicans, that figure increased to 24 percent. Exposure to Trump's quote about thugs in Baltimore produced a smaller increase (to 19 percent) that is not statistically distinct from the control group. Finally, one-fifth of respondents who were exposed to both quotations wrote something offensive or hateful about Mexicans. This was also not statistically distinct from the control group.

The right-hand plot in Figure 8 shows how frequently respondents wrote offensive or hateful things about millennials in each of the four conditions. Of comments written about millennials in the control condition, 19 percent were classified as offensive, compared to 22 percent in the groups that saw the "thugs" quote or both quotes and 25 percent in the group that was only exposed to the quote about Mexicans. The difference between the latter group and the control group was statistically significant, and the 6-point difference is quite

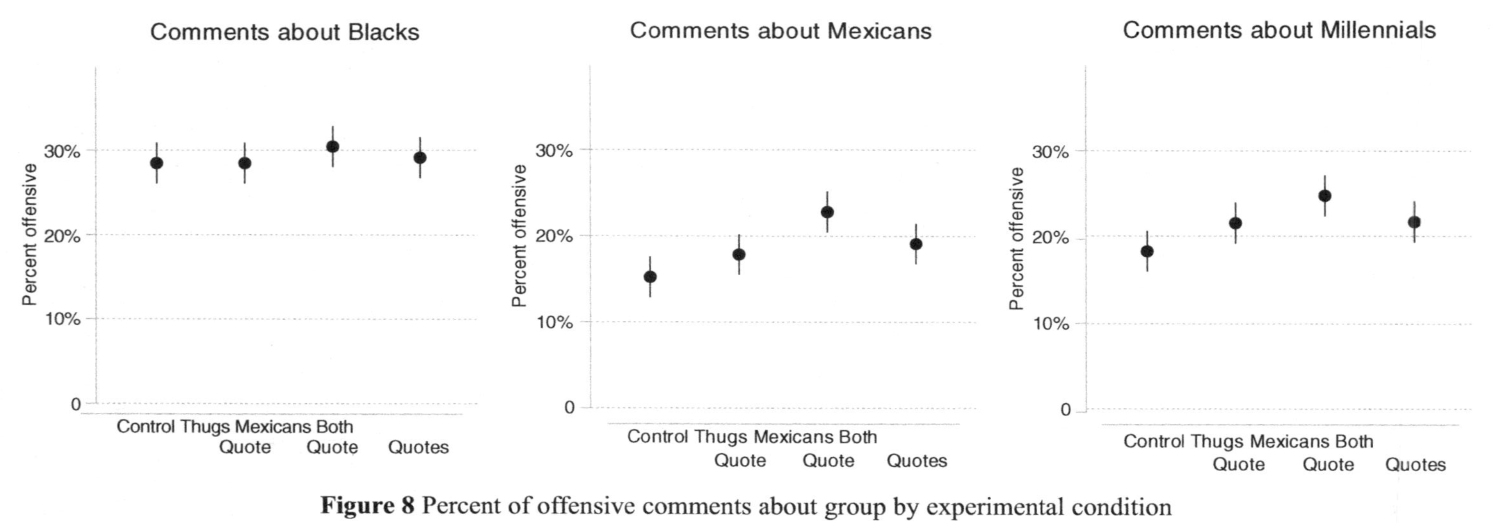

Figure 8 Percent of offensive comments about group by experimental condition

Note: Vertical lines represent 84 percent confidence intervals.

sizable, as it amounts to an increase in offensiveness of about one-third over the baseline.

Overall, there are two important patterns from Figure 8. First, it is Trump's quote about Mexicans (rather than his quote about African Americans) that appears to have the strongest influence on what respondents write about other groups. This pattern is likely due to the fact that the quote about Mexicans is especially offensive. Second, the effect of Trump's quote about Mexicans does not appear to be confined to the way in which respondents talked about Mexicans. Respondents who received this quote were also more likely to write offensive things about Millennials. This suggests that norm-breaking rhetoric from elites might have consequences beyond how citizens talk about the particular group that was targeted by the elite.

To provide a bit more context on the nature of the offensive comments given by white Americans in the experiment, Figure 9 shows the most common word stems used in the comments that were flagged as offensive or hateful by the coders.[17] The first panel shows that many of the most common words used in offensive comments about blacks evoke negative stereotypes toward African Americans – for example, words like "lazy," "violent," and "entitled" were often used by whites. Frequently, the offensive comments from whites also referred to blacks as being manipulated by Democrats, complaining too much, blaming others for their problems, being racist against whites, and taking advantage of the welfare system.

The second panel shows the common words used in offensive comments about Mexicans. Illegal was the most common word used by far, but these offensive comments also included references to drug use, being poor, and not speaking English. Finally, the offensive comments about millennials generally referred to the group as being "lazy," "spoiled," "entitled," "stupid," and "self-involved." In other words, the most typical offensive comments about millennials focused on words that were largely unrelated to Trump's quotes (which generally focused on violence and criminal behavior).

An examination of the words used by respondents also raises the question of whether respondents were simply parroting back words that they had just heard from Trump. Table 2 shows the incidence with which respondents used words that they were exposed to in Trump's quotes. The first row indicates the percentage of respondents who used a word to describe either blacks, Mexicans, or millennials that were also words that Trump used in his quote about Mexicans (e.g., "drugs," "crime," and "rapists"). Of respondents, 4.4 percent who were not exposed to Trump's quote about Mexicans used words that

[17] These are the comments that at least half of the coders tagged as offensive or hateful.

Table 2 Respondents' usage of words from Trump quotations, 2016 experiment

Terms	Not exposed to quote	Exposed to quote	Difference
rap*/drug*/crim*	4.4%	5.6%	1.2%
	(0.9)	(0.9)	(1.3)
thug*	0.3%	1.5%	1.2%
	(0.2)	(0.5)	(0.6)

Note: Entries are percentage of respondents using a word with the indicated stems. Columns identify whether respondents were exposed to a Trump quotation that included words with those same stems. Standard errors in parentheses.

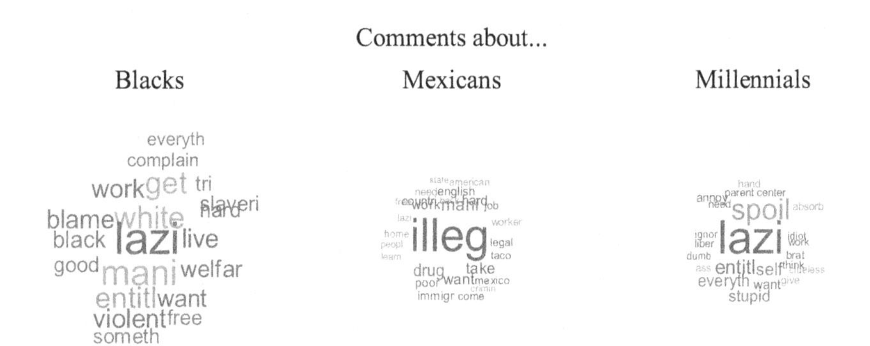

Figure 9 Most commonly used words in offensive comments

Trump used in his quotations about Mexicans, whereas 5.6 percent of those who received Trump's quote used these words in their own remarks. Thus, those receiving the Trump quote were 1.2 points more likely to use words that appear in that quote; however, this difference is relatively small and not statistically significant. Given that offensive comments about Mexicans increased by 8 points when respondents were exposed to Trump's quote, simple mimicry is only a very small share of that total difference.

The second row of results in Table 2 compares the incidence of the use of the stem "thug" among respondents who did and did not receive Trump's quote referring to African Americans as "thugs." Once again, we see that those receiving Trump's quote used the term 1.2 points more frequently than those who did not.

4.4 The Role of Partisanship and Motivation to Control Prejudice

So far, I have shown that exposure to Trump's quote about Mexicans makes people more likely to write offensive things about Mexicans and millennials.

But which people are most affected by his comments? Once again, I examine whether affinity for Trump is key.

Figure 10 produces separate estimates for respondents who identified as Trump versus Clinton voters.[18] Across the board, white Trump voters were more likely to write offensive things about each of the three groups when compared to white Clinton voters. However, we also see some evidence that Trump voters were more likely to react to being exposed to his prejudiced quotations. For example, the middle panel shows that Trump voters (but not Clinton voters) exposed to the quote about Mexicans were significantly more likely to write something offensive about Mexicans in response. Indeed, the treatment effect among Trump voters was approximately 10 percentage points when exposed only to the quote about Mexicans. By contrast, Clinton voters in the Mexicans quote condition were not significantly more likely to write an offensive comment about Mexicans. Once again, partisan motivations appear to play a central role in who responds to Trump's rhetoric.

As noted earlier, people may have different understandings of the norms regarding expressions of prejudice, and, likewise, people may be more or less motivated to follow those norms. To the extent that Trump's quotations affect how people perceive the norms around what is and is not acceptable to say about out-groups, we would expect this to matter most for people who are more motivated to control prejudice.

The 2016 CCES module included a battery of items aimed at measuring an individual's external motivation to respond without prejudice. These items ask respondents whether they agree or disagree with statements such as "I try to appear nonprejudiced to avoid disapproval from others." The idea is to attempt to separate respondents based on which individuals monitor their own prejudice due to a desire to appear nonprejudiced to others and which individuals are less concerned with such a goal (Plant & Devine 1998). If Trump's quotations are sending signals about norms regarding how much prejudice is acceptable to express, then we would likely find that the treatment effects would be most pronounced among those who have high levels of external motivation to express prejudice. After all, it is this group of individuals for whom perceived norms are mostly likely to make a difference, whereas those who have lower levels of motivation to hide prejudice will presumably care less about what norms prescribe.

The items asked in the survey were included for my colleagues' projects and thus were not perfectly designed for the purpose for which I apply them here. On the preelection survey, two of the three items asked specifically about external

[18] This variable is coded the same way as in the results presented in the previous section.

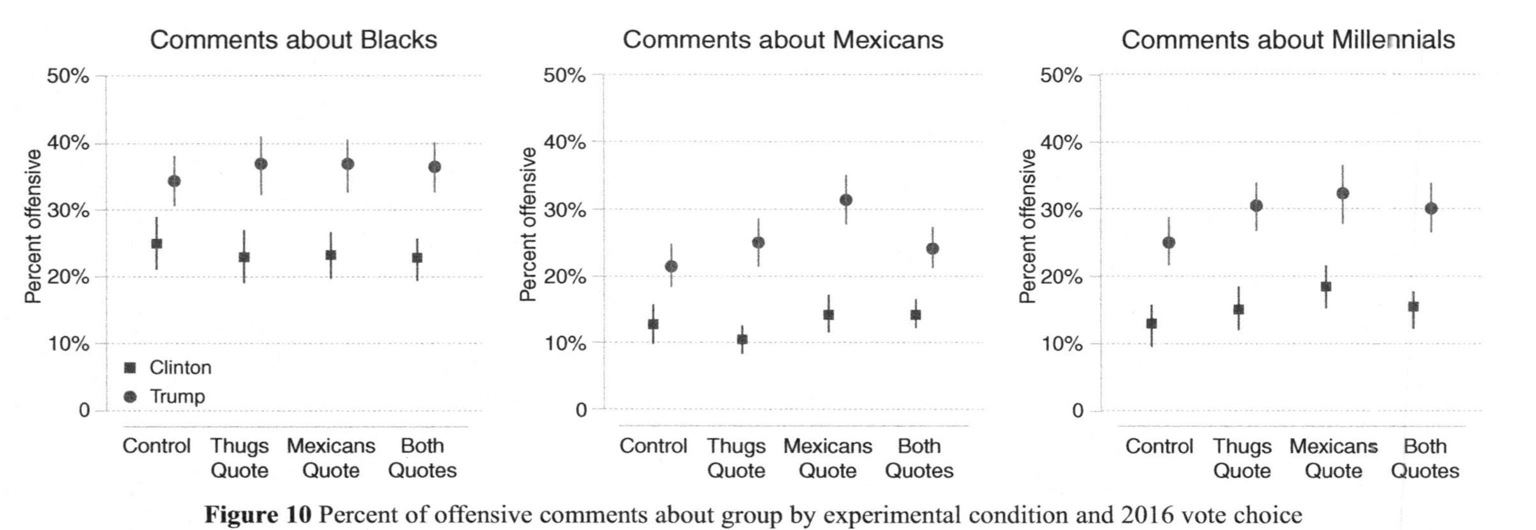

Figure 10 Percent of offensive comments about group by experimental condition and 2016 vote choice

Note: Vertical lines represent 84 percent confidence intervals.

pressure to control prejudice toward Muslims; on the postelection wave, some respondents answered items oriented toward Latinos, while others were asked about motivations to control prejudice toward blacks. I scaled all of the items together to create a single measure meant to capture each respondent's external motivation to control prejudice in general.[19] I then divided them into three groups. People with low external motivation to control prejudice were those who disagreed, on average, with statements like "I try to appear nonprejudiced to avoid disapproval from others." The second group was made up of those who typically selected the middle category on the five-point scale; and the third group consisted of respondents who typically agreed with statements like the one above.

Figure 11 plots the percent of offensive comments based on a respondent's motivation to control prejudice and whether they were assigned to the control condition or any of the treatment conditions. I combine the treatment conditions in this plot in order to simplify the presentation and preserve statistical power. Starting with the panel on the left, we can see the significance of how an individual scores on the motivation to control prejudice scale. In the control condition, people who score low on the scale wrote something offensive about blacks about 33 percent of the time; by comparison, those who scored high on the scale only wrote an offensive comment about blacks 22 percent of the time. A similar pattern is clear in the third plot – people who score low on the external motivation to control prejudice scale are always the most likely to write offensive comments about millennials.

But what types of people altered their behavior most when exposed to Trump's prejudiced remarks? In the first plot, people who score at the bottom and in the middle of the suppression of prejudice scale are about as likely to write something offensive about blacks in the control condition as they are when exposed to Trump's xenophobic quotes. However, exposure to Trump's remarks produces a statistically significant increase in expressions of prejudice among those who score highest in their motivation to control prejudice. Specifically, those who are highly motivated to control prejudice were 8 percentage points more likely to write something offensive about blacks when first exposed to at least one of Trump's quotes.

A similar pattern is evident in the results for millennials. In this case, those scoring low in external motivation to control prejudice are unaffected by exposure to Trump's quotes; but those in the middle and high end of the scale become more likely to write something offensive about millennials when exposed to Trump's offensive remarks.

[19] Responses to these items were largely consistent regardless of which target group was named.

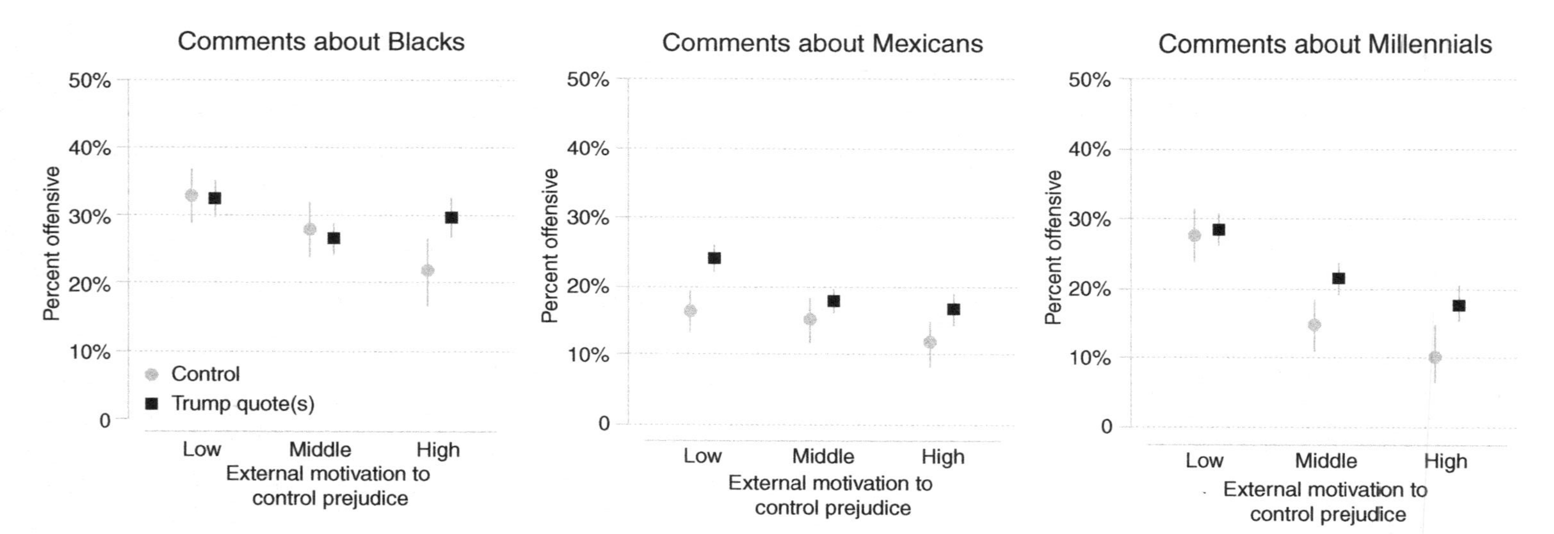

Figure 11 Percent of offensive comments about group by exposure to Trump quotations and level of motivation to suppress prejudice
Note: Vertical lines represent 84 percent confidence intervals.

The patterns for comments about Mexicans are somewhat different. First, in the control condition, external motivation to control prejudice is not a clear predictor of whether an individual wrote something offensive about Mexicans. That is, unlike with the other two groups, people were just as likely to write something offensive about Mexicans when they scored low on external motivation to control prejudice as when they scored high on that scale. Additionally, while all three groups were more likely to write something offensive when exposed to Trump's quotations, the difference was only significant for those with low motivation to control prejudice. It is not entirely clear why motivation to suppress prejudice operates differently for comments about Mexicans, though it is worth noting that people were less likely to write something offensive about this group than about blacks or millennials in the control condition. It may be that people who were referring to positive stereotypes of Mexicans in the absence of Trump's quote shifted to negative stereotypes when primed by Trump's quote. Indeed, many of the "positive" comments about Mexicans referred to them as being hardworking, whereas the negative comments were more about illegality and violence.

4.5 Results from a 2017 Experiment

In 2017, I ran a similar follow-up experiment. This time, however, I used different quotations as treatments in this experiment:

1 "If you have people coming out of mosques with hatred and death in their eyes and on their minds, we're going to have to do something."
2 "You could put half of Trump's supporters into what I call the 'basket of deplorables.' The racist, sexist, homophobic, xenophobic, Islamaphobic – you name it."

The first quotation is another from Trump during the 2016 campaign, but this time targeting Muslims. Including this quotation allows for a test of how people react when a different group is targeted. The second quote comes from Hillary Clinton. I included this quote to test for two potential effects. First, since the quotation is at least implicitly about white Americans, it may lead individuals to say more negative things about whites. Second, the quotation also is about calling out prejudice, and so being exposed to this quote might help to mitigate or reduce the extent to which people are willing to express their own prejudice about other groups (Munger 2017). As with the first experiment, respondents had a 50 percent chance of seeing each of these treatment statements; this means that about one-fourth of the sample (N = 154) saw no treatment statements; half saw one treatment statement (N = 165 and 168, respectively); and one-quarter saw both treatment statements (N = 169).

The 2017 experiment did not produce any statistically significant treatment effects. This may have been due to its relatively small sample size – only half as many respondents as in the 2016 experiment. It is also possible that, one year after Trump's election victory, much of his influence over people's expressions of prejudice may have already been felt. One important point is that Clinton's "deplorables" quote was not effective in reducing expressions of prejudice toward blacks or Muslims, suggesting that calling out such behavior may not be effective. This is a dynamic that I will test directly with the final experiment in Section 6.

4.6 Summary

This section presented a direct experimental test of the Trump effect – the notion that Trump's offensive and prejudicial rhetoric might cause individuals to express more prejudice toward out-groups. I find support for this expectation: specifically, individuals who were exposed to Trump's quote about Mexicans were significantly more likely to write offensive remarks, not only about Mexicans but also about millennials. The fact that I uncover significant effects for exposure to the quotation is especially noteworthy given the fact that many respondents had undoubtedly already heard Trump's quote before and may have already adjusted their expressions of prejudice accordingly. The likelihood that many had been "pre-treated" means that the effects uncovered here may represent a conservative estimate of the actual impact of Trump's rhetoric (Gaines, Kuklinski & Quirk 2006).

The evidence from these experiments is consistent with the notion that individuals took the offensive quotations as a cue about the norms regarding expressions of prejudice. First, very little mimicry was detected, indicating that people were not simply reusing the words that they had just heard. Second, exposure to the offensive quotation had the strongest impact among individuals who hide their prejudice from others.

However, the next experiment focuses more directly on the role of norms in this process. Specifically, that experiment uses as its dependent variable the extent to which respondents endorse norms related to the expression of prejudice. The experiment in the next section also examines whether this is merely a Trump-specific effect or if people are susceptible to being influenced by other politicians as well. The results will provide stronger confirmation not only for the theorized process regarding norms but also for the fact that the Trump effect is actually not at all limited to Trump himself.

5 How Elite Prejudice Alters Support for Norms

In the previous sections, I have shown that Trump supporters are less likely to object to sexist rhetoric when it is attributed to Trump and that they are more likely to write offensive things about identity groups when they are exposed to Trump's prejudiced rhetoric. However, while the experiments described thus far take advantage of "real-world" events to show how Trump's remarks affect how people talk about groups, there are several limitations. First, the experiments do not directly measure whether exposure to Trump's quotes is affecting respondents' perceptions about norms related to the expression of prejudice. That is, do people express more prejudice because they learn from Trump's statements that norms are more permissive than they assumed? Second, the experiment is focused on reactions to expressions of prejudice made by a single Republican politician, thereby raising questions about generalizability. Is this effect applicable to other politicians, including Democrats? And, third, the experiments exposed respondents to quotations that many had likely already heard.

In this section, I present results from an experiment designed to address these limitations. As will be described, the experiment involves exposing subjects to a politician justifying the telling of sexist or ethnic jokes. I use the topic of offensive jokes because previous research in social psychology has found that such jokes constitute a normative gray area with many people (Crandall, Eshleman & O'Brien 2002). Specifically, a series of studies found that when people are exposed to sexist humor they become more likely to express prejudice against women (Ford et al. 2008, 2001). This pattern occurs because the sexist humor shifts the local norms in a way that allows some to feel justified expressing prejudice toward women that they would otherwise suppress. Accordingly, this is a subject where signals from politicians may provide meaningful cues about whether such jokes are or are not appropriate.

Additionally, the evidence presented in this section focuses much more directly on the extent to which respondents endorse norms regarding the expression of prejudice. Specifically, I use items from scales developed by social psychologists meant to measure the degree to which an individual feels like it is important to appear nonprejudiced. These items ask, for example, about whether one should tell or laugh at racist, ethnic, or sexist jokes or use ethnic slurs. The aim is to more directly test the causal mechanism that I hypothesize is behind the Trump effect – whether elite expressions of prejudice cause people to shift their endorsement of norms against the expression of prejudice.

5.1 Design

This experiment was fielded on a module of the 2018 CCES preelection survey. The total sample size for this experiment was 1,109 non-Hispanic whites who were interviewed between September 27 and November 5, 2018. As with the previous survey experiments I have presented, this comes from a sample designed to be nationally representative of white Americans.

The manipulation involved randomly exposing some subjects to a quote from an unnamed politician who justified making inappropriate jokes. Subjects in the control condition (one-third of the sample) were not exposed to any quotation from the politician. The remaining two-thirds of respondents were randomly assigned to a treatment condition where they were told that a politician had recently justified taking part in either ethnic or sexist joke–telling. Specifically, the treatment groups saw text that read as follows:

> Recently, a [Democratic/Republican] politician said, "When other people are telling funny [ethnic/sexist] jokes, I might laugh and join in. It's the polite and social thing to do and there is nothing wrong with that."
>
> Did you happen to hear news about this?

The text inside the brackets (the party of the politician and the type of joke) was randomly assigned; this means that half of the subjects in the treatment group saw a quote referring to ethnic jokes and half saw a quote about sexist jokes. Similarly, half of the subjects saw a quote from a Democratic politician while the other half saw a quote from a Republican politician.

The immediate question asking subjects whether they had heard about this controversy was not the focus of the experiment.[20] Rather, the dependent variable for this experiment is the extent to which the respondent endorsed a set of statements meant to capture norms related to the expression of prejudice. These statements come from previous work in social psychology focusing on norms regarding expressions of prejudice. Three of the four items come from the Suppression of Prejudice Scale (SPS) developed by Crandall et al. (2002). This scale is particularly designed to measure one's "desire to appear nonprejudiced" (p. 370). The fourth statement from Zitek and Hebl (2007) is similarly designed to measure the clarity of social norms. For each statement, I include a citation to the study from which it originates.

- People should be able tell jokes that make fun of black people (Zitek & Hebl 2007).
- I don't want to appear racist or sexist, even to myself (Crandall et al. 2002).

[20] Owing to the fact that the story was fictional, only about 9 percent of respondents reported that they had heard about it.

- I won't use an ethnic slur, even if it's the word that pops into my head (Crandall et al. 2002).
- When other people are telling funny ethnic or sexist jokes, it is ok to laugh and join in (Crandall et al. 2002).

Respondents saw each of these statements one at a time and were asked to indicate the extent to which they agreed or disagreed with them on a five-point scale ranging from "strongly agree" to "strongly disagree."[21] The order in which the statements appeared was randomized, but the final statement was always shown last. The reason for keeping this item last among the list is that it most directly relates to the nature of the quotation in the treatment and including it earlier might have tipped off subjects to what the experiment was designed to capture.

In this section, I analyze the treatment effects on each of these statements individually as well as on a scale that combines responses to the four items into a single standardized score meant to capture the overall endorsement of anti-prejudice norms. I create the scale using an Item Response Theory graded response model; this produces a standardized score for each respondent with a mean of zero and a standard deviation of 1. Higher values on this scale indicate that the respondent more strongly endorses norms against the expression of prejudice.

Figure 12 shows how CCES respondents are distributed across values of this scale. One point worth noting is that nearly one-fifth of the non-Hispanic white respondents register the highest value on this scale, meaning they provided the response indicating the strongest endorsement against the expression of prejudice to all four items. The remaining respondents are scattered throughout the scale, with just a small share of respondents taking on the lowest possible value.

5.2 Results

As Figure 12 suggests, the modal response to each of the four items was to strongly endorse the position that was in opposition to expressions of prejudice. Specifically, 44 percent of people in the control group strongly disagreed that "people should be able to tell jokes that make fun of black people," and 33 percent strongly disagreed that "when other people are telling funny ethnic or sexist jokes, it is ok to laugh and join in." Additionally, 54 percent of control group respondents strongly agreed with the statement "I don't want to appear

[21] One additional item was included in this battery, but, because it did not load with the other four items, it is excluded from the analysis. The fact that the item does not load with the others suggests that it is measuring something other than support for nonprejudiced norms. See the online supplementary materials for more detail.

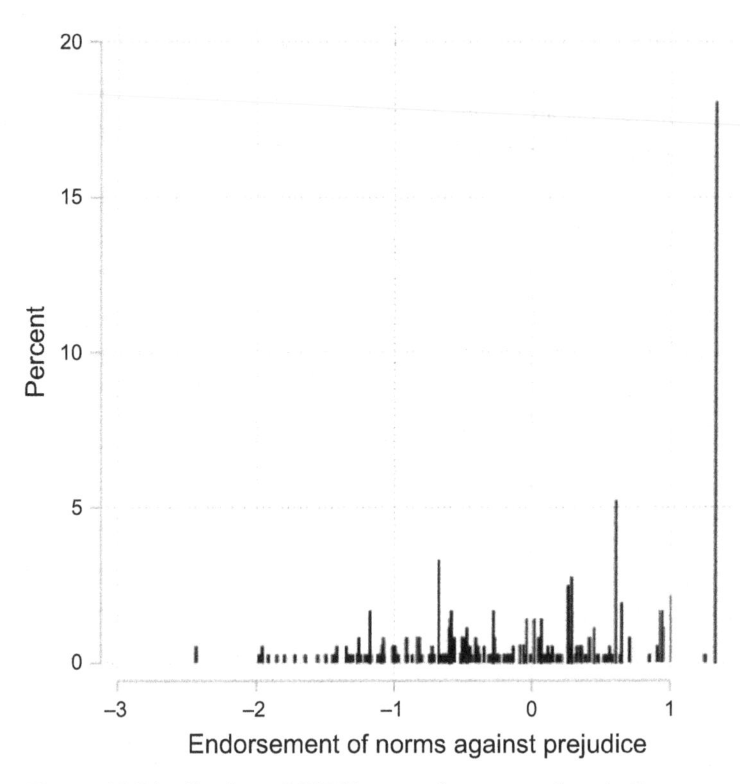

Figure 12 Distribution of CCES respondents on anti-prejudice norm endorsement scale

racist or sexist, even to myself," and 58 percent strongly agreed that "I won't use an ethnic slur, even if it's the word that pops into my head." Accordingly, I focus on changes in the percent of respondents selecting these categories when testing for treatment effects.

Figure 13 shows the percent of respondents strongly endorsing each norm based on their experimental condition. In this figure, I show the endorsement of norms for the ethnic joke treatment separately from the sexist joke treatment, but I do not (yet) separate the effects by the partisanship of the politician. Overall, the figure shows that the treatment effects are in the expected direction for each treatment and each item. However, it is the quotation focusing on ethnic jokes that produces larger and statistically significant reductions in norm endorsement. Specifically, on each item, non-Hispanic whites who were first shown the quotation from a politician saying that it is ok to laugh and join in when people are telling ethnic jokes were, on average, about 10 percentage points less likely to strongly endorse norms against the expression of prejudice. The largest effect size was on the statement "I don't want to appear racist or

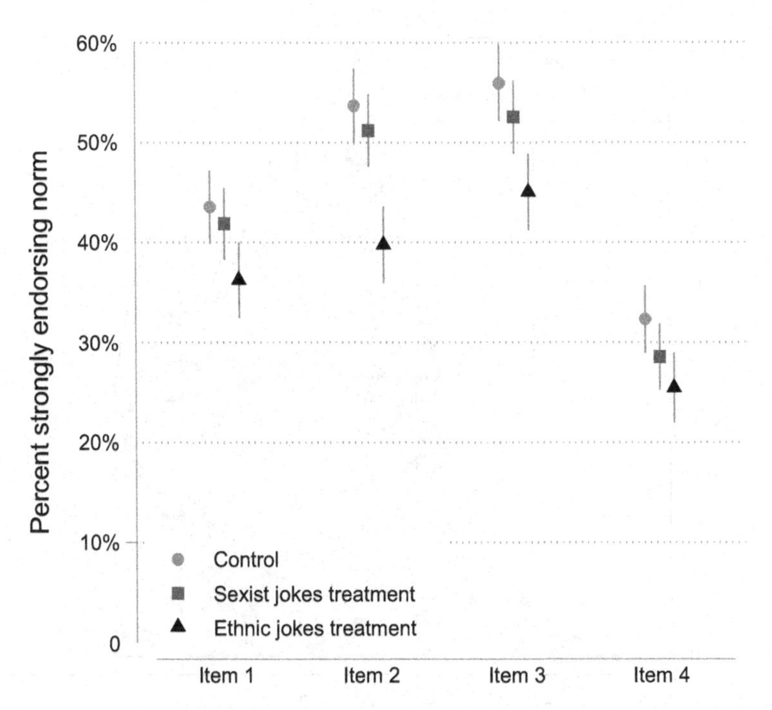

Figure 13 Percent strongly endorsing anti-prejudice norms by experimental condition

Note: Plot shows percent strongly (dis)agreeing with norm statements. Vertical lines represent 84 percent confidence intervals. Item 1 = "People should be able tell jokes that make fun of black people." Item 2 = "I don't want to appear racist or sexist, even to myself." Item 3 = "I won't use an ethnic slur, even if it's the word that pops into my head." Item 4 = "When other people are telling funny ethnic or sexist jokes, it is ok to laugh and join in."

sexist, even to myself." Respondents were 14 percentage points less likely to strongly agree with that statement when they were first exposed to the quotation from the politician. These effect sizes here are quite large, showing just how impressionable people are when it comes to their views on the norms regarding expressions of prejudice.

While Figure 13 shows the effects on each individual norm endorsement item, Figure 14 shows the distribution of individuals along the norm endorsement scale depending on whether they were in the control condition or in the condition which saw the quote about ethnic joke–telling. The light shaded area with a dotted line in the figure shows the distribution of respondents on the norm endorsement scale when they did not see any version of the quotation from the politician. The darker shaded area with a solid line shows the distribution for

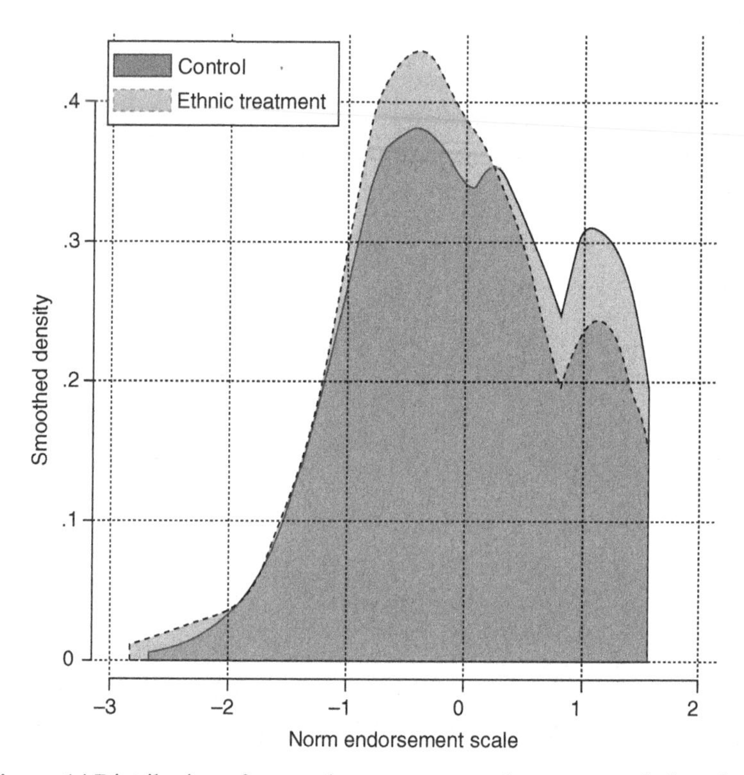

Figure 14 Distribution of respondents on norm endorsement scale based on assignment to control group or ethnic joke condition

those assigned to the condition where they read the quote from the politician justifying the telling of ethnic jokes. Comparing distributions provides more insight into who is most affected by the politician justifying expressions of prejudice. Namely, the proportion of respondents providing the strongest endorsements drops in the treatment condition, while the proportion of those in the middle of the distribution increases. In other words, some people who would otherwise be strong endorsers of norms against expressing prejudice become more ambivalent once they are exposed to the quote from the politician.

A formal test comparing the means from these distributions is statistically significant ($p = .034$). When a respondent was first shown the quote from the politician justifying the telling of ethnic jokes, their endorsement of anti-prejudice norms dropped by .15 standard deviations. In the summary to this section, I elaborate on possible reasons for why the politician's quote about ethnic jokes, but not about sexist jokes, significantly affected anti-prejudice norm endorsement.

Figure 15 shows the treatment effects of being exposed to the politician's quote about joining in on ethnic joke–telling conditional on the partisanship of the politician (which was randomly assigned) and the partisanship of respondents. I focus on the ethnic joke treatment since that is where we see the significant treatment effects in Figure 13.

Due to the relatively large confidence intervals, we cannot conclude much with certainty from the analysis in Figure 15. These large confidence intervals are partly a consequence of the fact that the sample size for this analysis is greatly reduced by limiting the focus to the ethnic quote treatment and restricting the analysis to partisans only. Among Republicans, the treatment effect of exposure to the politician's quote is relatively similar regardless of whether the politician is identified as a Democrat or a Republican. However, among Democrats, the treatment effect is fairly large when the quote is sourced to a Democratic politician (−.24, p = .068) but quite small when it is sourced to a Republican (−.03, p = .815). Thus, there is some indication that Democrats are more influenced by the treatment when it comes from a Democratic politician, but we cannot be confident in these effects. For Republicans, the party of the politician appears to make little difference.

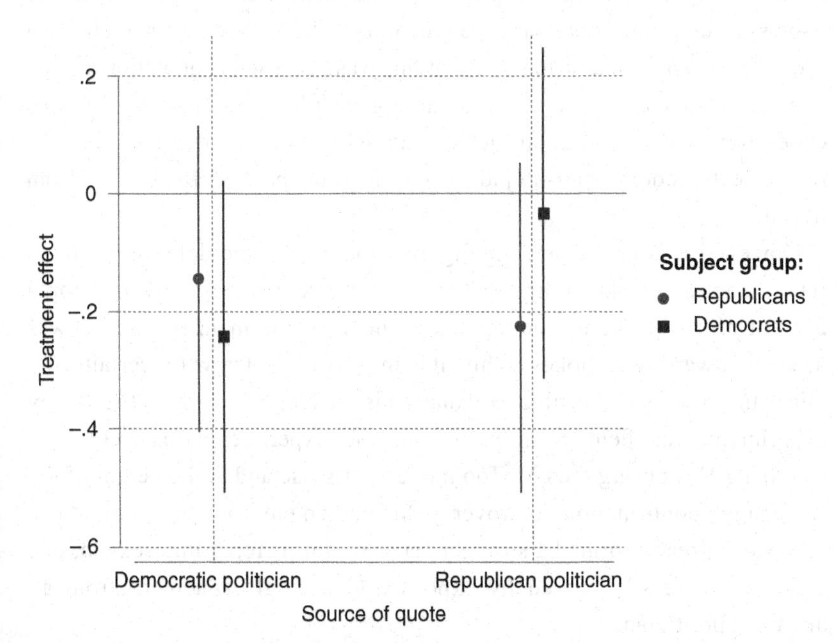

Figure 15 Treatment effects of exposure to politician's quote about ethnic jokes on anti-prejudice norm endorsement by partisanship

Note: Plot shows difference in anti-prejudice norm endorsement scale by party of respondent and randomly assigned party of politician. Vertical lines represent 95 percent confidence intervals.

5.3 Summary

Overall, the evidence from this experiment indicates that we can broaden claims about the Trump effect beyond just Trump himself. When individuals were exposed to a quotation in which a generic unnamed politician justified laughing at and joining in with ethnic joke–telling, they were significantly less likely to endorse norms against the expression of prejudice. Specifically, people exposed to this quotation were about 7 points less likely to strongly disagree with the statement "People should be able tell jokes that make fun of black people" or the statement "When other people are telling funny ethnic or sexist jokes, it is ok to laugh and join in." People seeing this quotation were also 14 points less likely to strongly agree with the statement "I don't want to appear racist or sexist, even to myself" and 11 points less likely to strongly agree with the statement "I won't use an ethnic slur, even if it's the word that pops into my head." In short, these respondents less strongly endorsed norms against the expression of prejudice.

A notable part of this experiment is the focus particularly on the endorsement of norms. While in the previous experiment I found that prejudiced quotes from politicians made people more likely to express their own prejudices, I was not able to show that this was because the quotation altered how people perceived the norms regarding such behavior. However, in this experiment I have shown that such quotations can, in fact, alter how strongly respondents endorse anti-prejudice norms. And these shifts are far from trivial.

However, it is also worth highlighting that it was the defense of ethnic rather than sexist joke–telling that produced these treatment effects. People did not react the the politician's quote in the same manner when it was directed toward sexist jokes. While it is impossible to know for certain why this is the case, one plausible explanation is the context in which the survey experiment was fielded. In particular, the experiment was fielded in October 2018, during the #MeToo movement's rise and at the height of the Kavanaugh confirmation controversy. In such an environment, individuals may have already formed a stronger sense of norms regarding sexism, one that was not easily moved by exposure to a single statement from an unnamed politician.

Of course, this raises a larger question of some significance – namely, whether politicians can counteract the effects of elite expressions of prejudice. In the following section, I present results from a final experiment designed to more rigorously answer this question.

6 Does Calling Out Prejudiced Rhetoric Work?

The experiments so far have shown clearly that, when people are exposed to politicians expressing prejudice or justifying joining in with such expressions, they are more likely to express prejudice themselves and to reduce the conviction with which they endorse anti-prejudicial norms. Overall, these findings paint a rather troubling picture of how much impact elite expressions of prejudice can have on the way that people talk about out-groups. But if elite expressions of prejudice can have such a powerful impact on how people behave, then perhaps people are just as willing to take signals when other elites criticize this behavior. In other words, are the effects that have been presented here mitigated when other elites call out the offending politician for expressing prejudice?

There is some existing research that suggests that such "calling out" actions can be effective under certain circumstances. For example, Munger (2017) conducted an innovative experiment in which Twitter accounts he controlled randomly sanctioned real accounts that were producing racist tweets. This sanctioning behavior was effective in reducing prejudiced tweets, but only when the sanctioning came from an account seemingly owned by a white male with many followers. However, a study by Banks and Hicks (2019) examined the effectiveness of sanctioning specifically related to Trump's rhetoric in 2016. They find that when politicians called out the racist nature of Trump's campaign it failed to undermine support for him among racially resentful whites, even when the sanctioning politicians were Republicans. Likewise, in their experiment focusing on the Trump effect, Newman et al. (2019) found that when other politicians condemned Trump's remarks it only had a minimal effect on suppressing expressions of prejudice.

Thus, it is unclear whether sanctioning, even from politicians of the same party, will mitigate the signals sent by political elites when it comes to expressions of prejudice. The following experiment, however, includes a randomization that will allow for a test of such "calling out" behavior in this context.

6.1 Design

The fourth and final experiment was fielded in February 2019. Subjects for this experiment were recruited via Lucid, which is a platform for online subjects that provides demographically and politically balanced samples to researchers (Coppock & McClellan 2019). However, unlike the YouGov surveys analyzed up to this point, the Lucid sample is not necessarily representative of American adults. A total of 3,029 adult subjects participated in the experiment.[22]

[22] I present the data for all respondents here, but see the online supplementary materials for analyses limited to just white subjects.

The design of this experiment builds on that from the one presented in the previous section. The treatment presents the same fictional quotation from a politician of a randomly assigned party. This time, I randomized whether the joke was sexist, ethnic, or racist (the racist condition was not part of the previous experiment). The key additional randomization in this experiment involved sanctioning from other politicians. Specifically, half of the subjects who saw the quote from the politician were also told that other Democrats or Republicans had said that the politician should apologize for the remarks. The party of the politicians demanding an apology was also randomized. Thus, the text this group saw was as follows:

> Recently, a [Democratic/Republican] politician said, "When other people are telling funny [racist/ethnic/sexist] jokes, I might laugh and join in. It's the polite and social thing to do and there is nothing wrong with that." [Following the remarks, many [Democratic/Republican] politicians said that these remarks were out of line and that the politician should apologize.] Did you happen to hear news about this?

As noted, this treatment allows for a test of whether the effects of the politician's statement would be blunted by other politicians calling out the remarks as inappropriate (Banks & Hicks 2019; Munger 2017).

Thus, about one-third of subjects were not exposed to any vignette; one-third saw a vignette featuring a politician saying that it is ok to make racist/ethnic/sexist jokes; and one-third received that vignette plus an additional sentence indicating that the politician had been rebuked for his remarks and called upon to apologize. As with the previous experiment, the immediate question asking subjects whether they had heard about this controversy was not the focus of the experiment.[23] Rather, the dependent variable is a question asked on the following screen, which was designed to capture the extent to which people endorse a norm against telling offensive jokes. On this screen, subjects were asked to indicate their agreement (on a five-point sale) with the statement "If a politician says that it is ok to make [racist/ethnic/sexist] jokes, they should apologize." The type of joke that the question asked about always matched the type of joke that the politician had referred to in the quotation on the previous screen. For subjects in the control condition who did not see the politician's quote, I randomly assigned the type of joke they were asked about.

Responses to this item provide a good measure of the extent to which individuals are willing to endorse a norm against engaging in offensive joke-telling. In some ways, this is a fairly low bar, since it is simply asking

[23] Owing to the fact that the story was fictional, only about 10 percent of subjects reported that they had heard about it.

respondents to agree with the action that the politicians are calling for. People who agree that the politician should apologize are signaling that this norm should be enforced, while those who respond neutrally or by disagreeing that the politician should apologize are failing to endorse the norm.

6.2 Results

Figure 16 shows the treatment effect of seeing the quote from the politician saying it is acceptable to make offensive jokes alongside the combined treatment effects of seeing that quote along with the rebuke from other politicians. The dependent variable here is the probability that a respondent strongly agrees that a politician should apologize for engaging in racist/ethnic/sexist jokes. I focus on the "strongly agree" response since it was the modal answer to the question and represents a strong endorsement of the norm against telling offensive jokes that is being conveyed in the rebuke treatment. This is also consistent with how I analyzed the previous experiment. However, the online supplementary materials show that the treatment effects are very similar when I focus instead on the mean response for the five-point scale.

In the control condition, 67 percent of subjects strongly agreed that a politician should apologize if they said it was acceptable to make racist jokes. However, when respondents were first subjected to a quotation from a politician saying that making such jokes is acceptable, just 57 percent strongly agreed with that statement. Accordingly, the treatment effect of seeing the quotation from the politician is about 10 percentage points ($p = .011$). When the politician's quotation was immediately followed by mention of a rebuke from other politicians, just 60 percent strongly agreed that the politician should apologize. Thus, the treatment effect for getting both the quotation and the rebuke is −8 percentage points ($p = .043$). This is only a marginally smaller treatment effect than what we observe when the quote is left unchallenged and the two treatment effects are not statistically distinct. Thus, the calling out and demand for an apology from other politicians appears to do little to dampen the effect of the original quotation on the subject's endorsement of norms.

The story is very much the same across the other joke conditions. Just 51 percent of respondents think that a politician should apologize for making ethnic jokes in the control condition; however, that drops to 40 percent in the treatment condition (treatment effect of −11 points, $p = .004$). Of control group respondents, 52 percent "strongly agreed" that a politician should apologize for engaging in sexist joke–telling, but this was just 42 percent among those who were exposed to the politician's quote (treatment effect of −9 points,

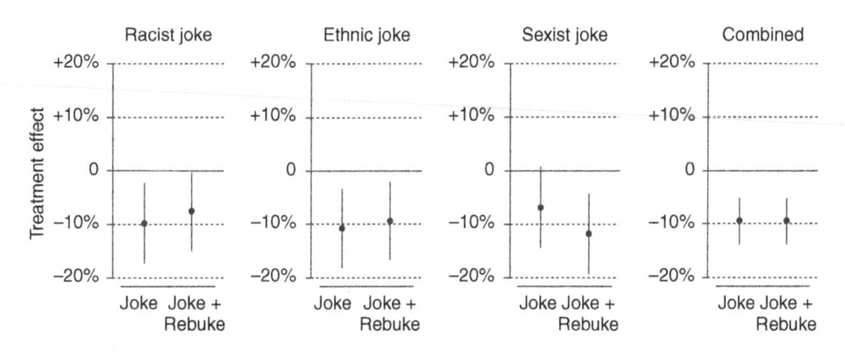

Figure 16 Treatment effect of politician quote and rebuke on strongly agreeing that politicians should apologize for making racist/ethnic/sexist jokes

Note: Plot shows difference between treatment condition of (1) seeing just the politician quote relative to control condition and (2) seeing the politician quote with the rebuke from other politicians on probability of strongly agreeing that politician should apologize. Vertical lines represent 95 percent confidence intervals.

p=.004). In both cases, the treatment effect was similar in magnitude and not statistically distinct when the politician's quote was followed by the rebuke.

Overall then, the treatment effects presented in Figure 16 are quite similar regardless of whether the joke was defined as racist, ethnic, or sexist. Given this robust finding across types of jokes, the final estimate in the figure combines subjects regardless of what type of joke they were asked about. The combined treatment effect is −9.5 points ($p < .001$) when subjects were just exposed to the politician's quote and −9.4 points ($p < .001$) when they saw both the quote and the rebuke. These remarkably similar treatment effects indicate that there is little evidence that having politicians call out the politician dampens the effect of his quotation on whether subjects endorse the norm against the expression of prejudice.

However, as noted, I randomized the party of the politician implicated, as well as the party of the politicians who offered a rebuke of that politician. This was designed to test whether people were motivated by partisanship in how they responded. It is possible that the rebuke has no net effect in Figure 16 because subjects from the same party follow the cue from the rebuke while those from the opposite party react strongly in the opposite direction. For example, if Democratic politicians demand that a Republican should apologize, then Republican subjects may actually be even less likely to agree that the politician should apologize in order to support their side in what has essentially become a partisan disagreement.

Figure 17 looks specifically at the treatment effect of the rebuke relative to seeing the politician's quote without the rebuke. To preserve power, I combine

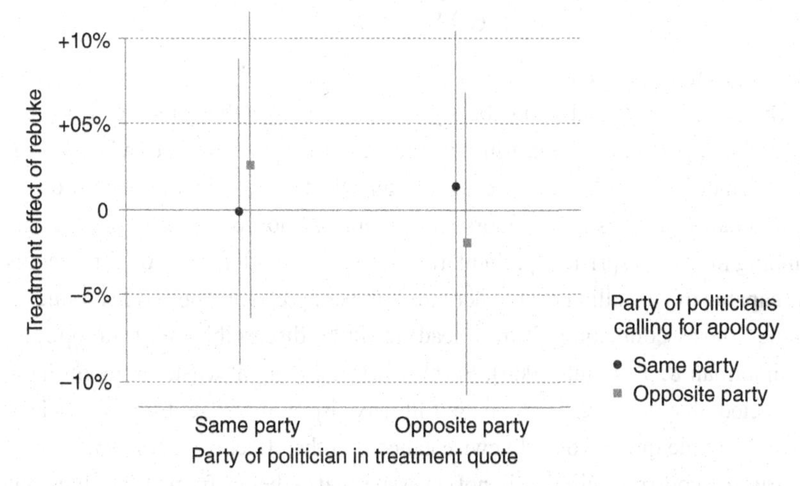

Figure 17 Treatment effects of call for apology conditional on party assigned to politician in quote and politicians calling for apology

Note: Plot shows treatment effect of seeing rebuke (compared to seeing the quote but no rebuke) based on whether the party of the quoted politician and the rebuking politicians are the same or different from the respondent's party. Vertical lines represent 95 percent confidence intervals.

the conditions across joke types, a decision that is justifiable given that the treatment effects plotted so far are quite similar across those three conditions (racist, ethnic, and sexist jokes). This figure breaks out the treatment effects based on the random assignment of party to the politicians in the vignette relative to the party affiliation of respondents. Specifically, the x-axis divides treatment effects based on whether the politician being quoted is of the same or opposite party from the subject. The circle and square dots indicate whether the politicians offering the rebuke are of the same or opposite party from the subject. Thus, for example, the first estimate plotted in the figure shows the estimated treatment effect when both the politician stating the original quotation and the politicians rebuking that politician are of the same party as the subject.

Notably, seeing the rebuke from other politicians produces small and non-statistically significant treatment effects regardless of the partisanship of the original politician or those offering the rebuke. It does not matter whether the politician offering the original quotation is from the opposite party and the rebuke comes from members of the subject's own party: the rebuke still has no discernible effect on whether the subject thinks politicians should apologize for engaging in offensive joke–telling. This is largely consistent with Banks and Hicks (2019) and Newman et al. (2019), who find that elite sanctioning had minimal (if any) effect.

6.3 Summary

In this section, I directly tested whether the negative effects that I documented earlier in this Element could be stymied by having other elites call out the prejudiced behavior. At least in this one experiment, I found no evidence that such sanctioning behavior reduces the impact of the original quotation on an individual's propensity to endorse anti-prejudice norms. On first glance, this finding may be surprising, particularly given that we often think of elite signals as capable of cancelling each other out. For example, when both sides frame an issue, those competing frames lead to little discernible shift in opinion (Sniderman & Theriault 2004). From this standpoint, at least, we might have expected that a prejudiced quote followed by a message from politicians criticizing the quote would likewise cancel out the effect of the quotation.

But, of course, prejudice is not an issue that is being framed by elites but rather an expression of something that people may or may not believe is wrong. In many ways, the ineffectiveness of the rebuke fits well with the idea that this is largely about people using these quotations as signals about norms. After all, the key theoretical mechanism I proposed at the outset is the notion that people hide some of their prejudice, but, when elites express prejudice themselves, it sends a signal to prejudiced people that it may be acceptable to reveal more than they previously thought. Once a politician effectively gives permission by expressing their own prejudice, the fact that others call that politician out may not make much of a difference. After all, the original quote signaled to our hypothetical prejudiced person that it is ok to express more prejudice, and perhaps all they have learned from the sanctioning by other politicians is that it is debatable whether what the original politician said was acceptable or not. In other words, the rebuke from other politicians may merely confirm that there is a gray area when it comes to expressions of prejudice. And it may very well be that all that is needed for one to justify the expression of their prejudice is to have the normative line between appropriate and inappropriate blurred by an authoritative source.

7 Conclusion

In this Element I have presented a litany of data focused on better understanding the Trump effect. This data included a nationally representative panel survey of American adults, as well as four different survey experiments focusing on how people react to elite expressions of prejudice. Because I have presented so much in a relatively limited amount of space, it may be useful to start with a summary of the findings and key contributions from each study. Table 3 presents such a summary.

Table 3 Summarizing the findings from each study

Study	Result	Contribution
Panel survey	Trump supporters agreed with sexist and anti-immigrant statements more after Trump's victory than they had before.	Suggests that people took Trump's victory as a cue that norms regarding expressions of prejudice are more permissive.
Experiment 1	Sexist Trump supporters express much less discomfort with sexist statements when they were attributed to Trump; sexist Trump opponents express much more discomfort with sexist statements when they were attributed to Trump.	Partisan motivations either reinforce (for Trump supporters) or counteract (for Trump opponents) expressions of prejudice.
Experiment 2	Whites write more offensive things about groups when first exposed to Trump's prejudiced quotes. Effects are generally stronger for those who are otherwise motivated to hide their prejudice.	Exposure to elite prejudice causes increased expressions of prejudice, especially among those who might otherwise be motivated to hide their prejudice from others.
Experiment 3	Whites less strongly endorse anti-prejudice norms after exposure to a politician's quote justifying expressions of prejudice.	The mechanism for elite influence does appear to be through whites' understandings of norms. Effect is not limited to rhetoric from Trump himself.
Experiment 4	When other politicians condemn a politician for expressing prejudice, it does not reduce the effects of the original quotation.	Calling out prejudice does not appear to solve the problem caused by the initial quotation.

Overall, the evidence is consistent with the notion that individuals take signals from politicians as cues about the norms related to expressions of prejudice. Why does this happen? For starters, messages from political elites are likely to be viewed as useful signals about norms because politicians have achieved their position as a result of having many people vote for them. If a politician who frequently expresses explicit prejudice is successful in the electoral arena, then it is reasonable for people to infer that the public is more accepting of prejudiced speech than they may have previously thought. Indeed, note from the panel survey data analysis presented in Section 2 that sexism and anti-immigrant prejudice increased among Trump supporters soon after he won the election. This is consistent with research by Crandall et al. (2018) showing that people's perceptions of norms regarding expressions of prejudice were more permissive after Trump's victory. Indeed, the third and fourth experiments were designed to directly test that mechanism. In those experiments, I focused specifically on whether respondents were willing to endorse anti-prejudice norms and found that, when they were exposed to a politician justifying expressions of prejudice, people responded by offering less support for the anti-prejudice norms in response.

Helping to fuel this process is partisanship. This can be seen most clearly in the first experiment, where individuals were exposed to sexist quotations that in one condition were attributed to an acquaintance but in another attributed to Trump. In the acquaintance condition, sexist Republicans expressed about the same level of discomfort with the statements as sexist Democrats. However, when these quotations were attributed to Trump, the evaluations of sexist respondents diverged: sexist Republicans expressed much lower levels of discomfort while sexist Democrats said they were more uncomfortable with the remarks. The process here is relatively simple – in the acquaintance condition, sexist Republicans were motivated to hide their own acceptance of the sexist remarks by saying that the remarks made them uncomfortable. However, in the Trump condition a second motivation was introduced – a motivation to show support for their preferred candidate. This counter-motivation led Trump supporters to reveal more acceptance of sexist remarks than they would have otherwise. The opposite happened for sexist Democrats – attributing the comments to Trump meant that sexist Democrats now had a motivation to express more discomfort with the statements.

This experiment helps to provide some context for longer-term trends that I discussed in Section 1 – specifically, the fact that white Democrats are increasingly giving more anti-racist and anti-xenophobic responses to survey questions, especially since Trump's election. As Sides et al. (2018) explain, "an important source of these shifts is almost certainly the backlash to Donald Trump himself and to his rhetoric and behavior as president" (p. 212). What appears to be happening is that Trump's open embrace of prejudice is leading many Democrats to reconsider the extent to which they are willing to endorse prejudicial statements themselves. Denying the existence of racism or being antagonistic toward women becomes much more difficult to stomach when a highly disliked political figure has made it such a central part of his brand. In short, people who strongly dislike Trump simply do not want to express the same kinds of sentiments toward out-groups as he so frequently does.

At the same time, Republican responses to survey items like this have shifted little, if at all. This suggests that Trump is not necessarily making his supporters more prejudiced. Yet, what the findings presented here (particularly those from the second experiment) suggest is that Trump may encourage his prejudiced supporters to be more explicit in how they talk about the groups they dislike. In short, many Trump supporters no longer feel as though they have to hide or moderate their hate.

Together, these patterns are symptomatic of a broader trend in which partisan polarization is increasingly defined by (and driven by) social identity (Mason 2018; Tesler 2016). This also helps to make sense of the simultaneous and contrasting influence that Trump has had on expressions of prejudice by the American public. On one side, white Democrats react to Trump's rhetoric by becoming more willing to acknowledge white privilege and less willing to endorse negative stereotypes about out-groups (Hopkins & Washington 2020). On the other side, white Republicans take Trump's rhetoric as permission to be more vocal and public about their prejudicial views. Together, these trends mean that partisan polarization is increasingly defined by a heated conflict over how Americans view women, people of color, and other salient identity groups.

Voters' racism and sexism both played a larger role in predicting their choices in 2016 than it had in previous elections (Schaffner et al. 2018; Sides et al. 2018; Valentino, Wayne & Oceno 2018). Two years later, racism and sexism were a stronger predictor of the House vote than they had been in 2016 (Schaffner, in press). And during Trump's presidency, so many of the key controversies have been directly about issues of identity – whether it be the travel ban on predominantly Muslim countries, the sexual assault allegations against Brett Kavanaugh, or the Black Lives Matter protests that followed the murder of George Floyd by Minneapolis police officers.

But if Trump is simply giving some of his supporters license to express things they are already thinking, and not necessarily changing their internal beliefs, then does it really matter? The answer is a resounding yes. For starters, norms help us get along in daily life without needlessly offending our friends, neighbors, and acquaintances. They help us avoid conflict, and they promote cooperation and compromise. But even more importantly, norms are aspirational. They show us how our own thoughts and feelings fall short of what society asks of us. If a person thinks something terrible about a group but understands that they cannot say it out loud, then that person is acknowledging that what they think is not widely accepted. And conceding that one's views are not mainstream can be an important step toward changing those views. Indeed, this appears to be what is happening with many white Democrats.

So what can be done? After all, the final experiment showed that having other politicians criticize a prejudiced statement did not blunt that statement's impact. This finding is consistent with other recent experiments that have likewise found minimal, if any, effect for condemnations of elite expressions of prejudice (Banks & Hicks 2019; Newman et al. 2019). Instead, it is useful to return to the main reason why people are so likely to take cues about norms from politicians – namely, that they can reasonably infer that the fact that those politicians have been successful means that support for their expressions of prejudice is widespread among their fellow citizens. It is easy to imagine that, if Trump's presidential campaign had been a clear failure, the influence of his prejudiced rhetoric would likely have been minimal.

Thus, the future of the Trump effect may hinge in part on whether Trump and other prejudice-expressing politicians continue to enjoy electoral success. On this front, there may be some cause for hope. In research conducted on the 2018 midterm elections, I found that "Trump's hostility toward women and minorities is becoming part of the Republican Party's brand and that this appeared to result in an electoral penalty for Republican candidates in 2018" (Schaffner, in press). There is even more hope in the immediate wake of the protests in response to the murder of George Floyd. Polls conducted in the weeks after the initial protests found that the percentage of white Americans who acknowledge the problem of racism increased markedly; much of this increase was even evident among white Republicans (Schaffner 2020).

If people take Trump's success as a signal about the acceptance of prejudiced rhetoric, then they would likely take his defeat – and the defeat of other prejudice- peddling politicians – as an equally strong counter-signal. Furthermore, such a defeat should also dissuade other politicians from following in Trump's footsteps. There is likely no easy path to restoring mass adherence to anti-prejudiced norms; it will instead come from the signals that Americans send when they decide what types of candidates, and what types of values, they are willing to support in the voting booth.

References

Allport, G. W. (1954). *The Nature of Prejudice*. Reading, MA: Addison-Wesley.

Banks, A. J., & Hicks, H. M. (2019). The effectiveness of a racialized counterstrategy. *American Journal of Political Science* 63(2): 305–322.

Becker, J. C. (2010). Why do women endorse hostile and benevolent sexism? The role of salient female subtypes and internalization of sexist contents. *Sex Roles* 62(7–8): 453–467.

Blanchard, F. A., Crandall, C. S., Brigham, J. C., & Vaughn, L. A. (1994). Condemning and condoning racism: A social context approach to interracial settings. *Journal of Applied Psychology* 79(6): 993.

Blanchard, F. A., Lilly, T., & Vaughn, L. A. (1991). Reducing the expression of racial prejudice. *Psychological Science* 2(2): 101–105.

Bullock, J. G. (2009). Partisan bias and the Bayesian ideal in the study of public opinion. *Journal of Politics* 71(03): 1109–1124.

Campbell, A., Converse, P., Miller, W., & Stokes, D. (1960). *The American Voter*. Chicago, IL: University of Chicago Press.

Cappella, J. N., & Jamieson, K. H. (1997). *Spiral of Cynicism: The Press and the Public Good*. Oxford: Oxford University Press.

Carey, J. M., Helmke, G., Nyhan, B., Sanders, M., & Stokes, S. (2019). Searching for bright lines in the Trump presidency. *Perspectives on Politics* 17(3): 699–718.

Chong, D., & Druckman, J. N. (2007). Framing theory. *Annual Review of Political Science* 10: 103–126.

Cialdini, R. B., & Trost, M. R. (1998). Social influence: Social norms, conformity and compliance. In *The Handbook of Social Psychology*, edited by D. T. Gilbert, S. T. Fiske & G. Lindzey, pp. 151–192. New York: McGraw-Hill.

Coppock, A., & McClellan, O. A. (2019). Validating the demographic, political, psychological, and experimental results obtained from a new source of online survey respondents. *Research & Politics* 6(1): 1–14.

Costello, M. B. (2016). *The Trump Effect: The Impact of the Presidential Campaign on Our Nation's Schools*. Montgomery, AL: Southern Poverty Law Center.

Crandall, C. S., & Eshleman, A. (2003). A justification-suppression model of the expression and experience of prejudice. *Psychological Bulletin* 129(3): 414.

Crandall, C. S., Eshleman, A., & O'Brien, L. (2002). Social norms and the expression and suppression of prejudice: The struggle for internalization.

Journal of Personality and Social Psychology 82(3): 359–378. doi:10.1037/0022–3514.82.3.359.

Crandall, C. S., Miller, J. M., & White, M. H. (2018). Changing norms following the 2016 US presidential election: The Trump effect on prejudice. *Social Psychological and Personality Science* 9(2): 186–192. doi:1948550617750735.

Crosby, F., Bromley, S., & Saxe, L. (1980). Recent unobtrusive studies of black and white discrimination and prejudice: A literature review. *Psychological Bulletin* 87(3): 546.

Dovidio, J. F., & Gaertner, S. L. (1986). *Prejudice, Discrimination, and Racism.* Cambridge, MA: Academic Press.

Druckman, J., & Bolsen, T. (2011). Framing, motivated reasoning, and opinions about emergent technologies. *Journal of Communication* 61(4): 659–688. doi:10.1111/j.1460-2466.2011.01562.x.

Edwards, G. S., & Rushin, S. (2018). The effect of President Trump's election on hate crimes. SSRN 3102652.

Engelhardt, A. M. (2018). Racial attitudes through a partisan lens. *British Journal of Political Science*: 1–18. doi:10.1017/S0007123419000437.

Ford, T. E., Boxer, C. F., Armstrong, J., & Edel, J. R. (2008). More than "just a joke": The prejudice-releasing function of sexist humor. *Personality and Social Psychology Bulletin* 34(2): 159–170.

Ford, T. E., Wentzel, E. R., & Lorion, J. (2001). Effects of exposure to sexist humor on perceptions of normative tolerance of sexism. *European Journal of Social Psychology* 31(6): 677–691.

Gaines, B. J., Kuklinski, J. H., & Quirk, P. J. (2006). The logic of the survey experiment reexamined. *Political Analysis* 15(1): 1–20.

Gervais, B. T. (2014). Following the news? Reception of uncivil partisan media and the use of incivility in political expression. *Political Communication* 31 (4): 564–583.

Gervais, B. T. (2015). Incivility online: Affective and behavioral reactions to uncivil political posts in a web-based experiment. *Journal of Information Technology & Politics* 12(2): 167–185.

Glick, P., & Fiske, S. T. (1996). The ambivalent sexism inventory: Differentiating hostile and benevolent sexism. *Journal of Personality and Social Psychology* 70(3): 491.

Gross, J. H., & Johnson, K. T. (2016). Twitter taunts and tirades: Negative campaigning in the age of Trump. *PS: Political Science & Politics* 49(4): 748–754.

Hopkins, D. J., & Washington, S. (2020). The rise of Trump, the fall of prejudice? Tracking white americans' racial attitudes 2008–2018 via a panel survey. *Public Opinion Quarterly* 84(1): 119–140.

Huddy, L., Mason, L., & Aarøe, L. (2015). Expressive partisanship: Campaign involvement, political emotion, and partisan identity. *American Political Science Review* 109(1): 1–17.

Hurwitz, J., & Peffley, M. (1992). Traditional versus social values as antecedents of racial stereotyping and policy conservatism. *Political Behavior* 14 (4): 395–421.

Iyengar, S., Sood, G., & Lelkes, Y. (2012). Affect, not ideology: A social identity perspective on polarization. *Public Opinion Quarterly* 76(3): 405–431.

Julious, S. A. (2004). Using confidence intervals around individual means to assess statistical significance between two means. *Pharmaceutical Statistics: The Journal of Applied Statistics in the Pharmaceutical Industry* 3(3): 217–222.

Kalkan, K. O., Layman, G. C., & Uslaner, E. M. (2009). "Bands of others"? Attitudes toward Muslims in contemporary American society. *Journal of Politics* 71(3): 847–862.

Kuklinski, J. H., Cobb, M. D., & Gilens, M. (1997). Racial attitudes and the "New South." *Journal of Politics* 59(2): 323–349.

Kunda, Z. (1990). The case for motivated reasoning. *Psychological Bulletin* 108 (3): 480–498.

Levitsky, S., & Ziblatt, D. (2018). *How Democracies Die*. New York: Broadway Books.

Mason, L. (2016). A cross-cutting calm: How social sorting drives affective polarization. *Public Opinion Quarterly* 80(S1): 351–377.

Mason, L. (2018). *Uncivil Agreement: How Politics Became Our Identity*. Chicago, IL: University of Chicago Press.

Mason, L., & Wronski, J. (2018). One tribe to bind them all: How our social group attachments strengthen partisanship. *Political Psychology* 39(S1): 257–277.

Mendelberg, T. (2001). *The Race Card: Campaign Strategy, Implicit Messages, and the Norm of Equality*. Princeton, NJ: Princeton University Press.

Munger, K. (2017). Tweetment effects on the tweeted: Experimentally reducing racist harassment. *Political Behavior* 39(3): 629–649.

Mutz, D. C. (2006). *Hearing the Other Side: Deliberative versus Participatory Democracy*. Cambridge: Cambridge University Press.

Newman, B., Merolla, J. L., Shah, S., Lemi, D. C., Collingwood, L., & Ramakrishnan, S. K. (2019). The Trump effect: An experimental investigation of the emboldening effect of racially inflammatory elite communication. *British Journal of Political Science*: 1–22. doi:10.1017/S0007123419000590.

Nithyanand, R., Schaffner, B., & Gill, P. (2017). Online political discourse in the Trump era. *arXiv preprint*. Available at: arXiv:1711.05303.

Paluck, E. L. (2009). Reducing intergroup prejudice and conflict using the media: A field experiment in Rwanda. *Journal of Personality and Social Psychology* 96(3): 574.

Paluck, E. L., & Green, D. P. (2009). Prejudice reduction: What works? a review and assessment of research and practice. *Annual Review of Psychology* 60: 339–367.

Petersen, M. B., Skov, M., Serritzlew, S. R., & Ramsøy, T. (2013). Motivated reasoning and political parties: Evidence for increased processing in the face of party cues. *Political Behavior* 35: 831–854. doi:10.1007/s11109-012-9213-1.

Plant, E. A., & Devine, P. G. (1998). Internal and external motivation to respond without prejudice. *Journal of Personality and Social Psychology* 75(3): 811.

Roese, N. J., & Jamieson, D. W. (1993). Twenty years of bogus pipeline research: A critical review and meta-analysis. *Psychological Bulletin* 114(2): 363.

Rokeach, M., & Ball-Rokeach, S. J. (1989). Stability and change in American value priorities, 1968–1981. *American Psychologist* 44(5): 775.

Schaffner, B. F. (2020). "White Republicans and Independents are starting to acknowledge their privilege, but will it last?" www.dataforprogress.org/blog/2020/6/15/white-republicans-and-independents-are-starting-to -acknowledge-their-privilege-but-will-it-last.

Schaffner, B. F. (in press). The heightened importance of racism and sexism in the 2018 US midterm elections. *British Journal of Political Science*.

Schaffner, B. F., MacWilliams, M., & Nteta, T. (2018). Understanding white polarization in the 2016 vote for president: The sobering role of racism and sexism. *Political Science Quarterly* 133(1): 9–34.

Schaffner, B. F., & Sellers, P. J. (2009). *Winning with Words: The Origins and Impact of Political Framing*. Abingdon: Routledge.

Sides, J., Tesler, M., & Vavreck, L. (2018). *Identity Crisis: The 2016 Election and the Battle for the Meaning of America*. Princeton, NJ: Princeton University Press.

Sigall, H., & Page, R. (1971). Current stereotypes: A little fading, a little faking. *Journal of Personality and Social Psychology* 18(2): 247.

Sniderman, P. M., & Theriault, S. M. (2004). "The structure of political argument and the logic of issue framing." In *Studies in Public Opinion: Attitudes, Nonattitudes, Measurement Error, and Change*, edited by W. E. Saris and P. M. Sniderman, pp. 133–165. Princeton, NJ: Princeton University Press.

Taber, C., & Lodge, M. (2006). Motivated skepticism in the evaluation of political beliefs. *American Journal of Political Science* 50(3): 755–769.

Tajfel, H., & Turner, J. C. (1979). An integrative theory of intergroup conflict. *Social Psychology of Intergroup Relations* 33(47): 74.

Tesler, M. (2016). *Post-racial or Most-racial? Race and Politics in the Obama Era*. Chicago, IL: University of Chicago Press.

Valentino, N. A., Neuner, F. G., & Vandenbroek, L. M. (2018). The changing norms of racial political rhetoric and the end of racial priming. *Journal of Politics* 80(3): 757–771.

Valentino, N. A., Wayne, C., & Oceno, M. (2018). Mobilizing sexism: The interaction of emotion and gender attitudes in the 2016 US presidential election. *Public Opinion Quarterly*, 82(suppl. 1): 213–235.

Weeks, B. E. (2015). Emotions, partisanship, and misperceptions: How anger and anxiety moderate the effect of partisan bias on susceptibility to political misinformation. *Journal of Communication* 65(4): 699–719.

Yglesias, M. (2019). The great awokening. *Vox*, March 22. www.vox.com/2019/3/22/18259865/great-awokening-white-liberals-race-polling-trump-2020.

Zaller, J. (1992). *The Nature and Origins of Mass Opinion*. Cambridge: Cambridge University Press.

Zitek, E. M., & Hebl, M. R. (2007). The role of social norm clarity in the influenced expression of prejudice over time. *Journal of Experimental Social Psychology* 43(6): 867–876.

Acknowledgements

I thank the University of Massachusetts Amherst and Tufts University for funding the data collection for this research. I also thank the National Science Foundation for its support of the Cooperative Congressional Election Study (award numbers 1559125 and 1756447). This project has benefited from the input of a large number of colleagues (too many to list individually). In particular, I received helpful comments from the American Politics Working Group at UMass, the Social Psychology Brown Bag group at UMass, the Identity Politics Research Group, attendees at Cornell University's series on "Politics and Justice in the Era of Donald Trump," the Program in Quantitative Social Science at Dartmouth College, and discussants at the American Political Science Association and Midwest Political Science Association conferences, including Paul Goren, Katherine McCabe, and Stephen Medvic. Finally, I especially thank Tatishe Nteta, Justin Gross, Scott Blinder, Jesse Rhodes, and Mia Costa for giving sustained feedback on this project since its inception.

Cambridge Elements

American Politics

Advisory Board

About the series

The Cambridge Elements Series in *American Politics* publishes authoritative contributions on American politics. Emphasizing works that address big, topical questions within the American political landscape, the series is open to all branches of the subfield and actively welcomes works that bridge subject domains. It publishes both original new research on topics likely to be of interest to a broad audience and state-of-the-art synthesis and reconsideration pieces that address salient questions and incorporate new data and cases to inform arguments.

Cambridge Elements

American Politics

Elements in the series

Policy Success in an Age of Gridlock: How the Toxic Substances Control Act Was Finally Reformed
Lawrence S. Rothenberg

Roll Call Rebels: Strategic Dissent in the United States and United Kingdom
Justin H. Kirkland, Jonathan B. Slapin

Legislative Hardball: The House Freedom Caucus and the Power of Threat-Making in Congress
Matthew Green

Red, Green, and Blue: The Partisan Divide on Environmental Issues
David Karol

Contemporary US Populism in Comparative Perspective
Kirk Hawkins, Levente Littvay

False Alarm: The Truth about Political Mistruths in the Trump Era
Ethan Porter, Thomas J. Wood

Converging on Truth: A Dynamic Perspective on Factual Debates in American Public Opinion
James A. Stimson, Emily Wager

A full series listing is available at: www.cambridge.org/core/series/elements-in-american-politics

Printed in the United States
By Bookmasters